Carver Alan Ames was born in Ireland in 1953. His childhood and adulthood were turbulent. He married Kathryn and moved to Australia and raised two children. Then in 1993, angels, saints, and the Holy Trinity began communicating with him.

At that time, he experienced a mini-judgment, and fell totally in love with Jesus. From a violent man, he has become child-like with a complete devotion to God. Alan and his wife left their jobs in August of 1996 to devote their time fully to do God's work, founding the Touch of Heaven ministry.

Books Also Available From:

New Zealand
Patrick J. Clegg
P. O. Box 31495
Lower Hutt
New Zealand
Phone & Fax: 644 566 5786

England
Angelus Communications
22 Milbury Drive
Littleborough
Lancashire OL15 OBZ
England
Phone & Fax: 01706 372 674

Ireland
Touch of Heaven
66 Landscape Park
Churchtown
Dublin 14, Ireland
Phone & Fax: 01-298 5403

Australia
Touch of Heaven
P. O. Box 85
Wembley
Western Australia 6014
Phone 09-275 6608
Fax: 619-382 4392

The decree of the Congregation for the Propagation of the Faith A.A.S.58, 1186 (Approved by Pope Paul VI on October 14, 1966) states that the Nihil Obstat and Imprimatur are no longer required on publications that deal with private revelations, provided that they contain nothing contrary to faith and morals.

The publisher recognizes and accepts that the final authority regarding the events described in this book rests with the Holy See of Rome, to whose judgment we willingly submit.

DEDICATION

This book is dedicated to those who have done so much to help me:
Russel & Enid Fonceca
George & Linda Martinskis
Sr. Claude MacNamara
John & June Murphy
Richard & Judy Priestley
and to Father Gerard Dickinson,
who has helped me more than he knows.

ISBN No. 0 646 27605 0

1st Printing in Australia, 1995—7,000 copies
2nd Printing in U.S.A., 1997—15,000 copies

Printed and available in the U.S.A. by:
The 101 Foundation, Inc.
Asbury, New Jersey 08804
Phone: 908-689 8792
Fax: 908-689 1957

PREFACE

I was asked by the writer of this book, Carver Alan Ames, to write the preface.

As a Catholic priest, I would like to tell you that I am astonished and, at the same time, impressed with the spiritual and ascetic knowledge of this man.

Bear in mind that Alan Ames has never studied Philosophy, Theology, or Mariology. Analysing this book, I did not find anything which offends or obscures the teachings of the Church with regard to faith or morals. No wonder he has the permission of our Archbishop of Perth to speak in halls or churches, wherever he is invited to go.

In his writings, Alan often says, "Our Mother Mary told me to write this," or "Jesus Christ inspired me to describe such and such a thought."

He is often helped by the Son, Jesus, the Father and the Holy Spirit. Alan's words or writings come spontaneously from his genuine heart that only a man of God or a man of prayer can arrive at to such an extent.

His presence, while talking publicly, attracts a large number of faithful and sceptical people who come to listen to what he says. Similarly, through his writings there have been conversions, as he and his beloved wife were converted not so long ago. As a holy man, Alan is also gifted by God while praying over people.

I encourage people to read whatever Alan has already published, but in a special way this book, that I have read very closely, which has greatly increased my spirituality. May God and Mary bless you all.

Fr. Lawrence J. Attard, K.O.S.J.
October 16, 1995

Editor's Note

Alan Ames is a gifted and unique man for many reasons. God has chosen him to receive visions and locutions, but Alan has also been given the gift of a child-like truth and honesty that draws people to him in a warm and loving way. To me, this particular quality makes what he says credible and profound. It is like the sincerity and simplicity found in a child, which all too often is lost in adulthood.

This book of visions and messages was written before Alan started to see the life of Jesus in February of 1996, which, when printed, was titled *"Through the Eyes of Jesus."* However, in a different and important way, *Messages to Alan Ames* tells us how to live...how to become a saint, which is the only true vocation of every human being.

When I first saw a picture of Our Lady of the Cross, as Our Lady showed herself to Alan, I was concerned that Our Lady had the Scapular tied around her waist instead of wearing it around her neck. As an avid promoter of the brown Scapular, this seemed to me to be inappropriate, since we always encourage people that to receive the full benefit of this sacramental, one must wear it around one's neck.

Then I spoke to Dr. Courtenay Bartholomew, Professor of Medicine and a renowned medical and Marian researcher, and he pointed out that it would not be proper protocol for Our Lady to be wearing the scapular around her neck. At Garabandal, she is seen with the scapular around her wrist. At Carmel, both she and Jesus are seen with a scapular in their hands, holding it out to us. Sister Christina Marie Griggs, O. Carm., Associate Provincial Directress of Lay Carmelites in the U.S., told me Our Lady carries, holds, or wears the brown scapular to tell us that *she wants us to wear it.*

I see now that this is one of the visible messages of Our Lady of the Cross. There are others which are also very important. Read on to what the Trinity and Our Lady disclose through Alan Ames, a privileged soul. And now, you, by reading this book, also become a privileged soul. God bless you.

Dr. Rosalie A. Turton, Editor

Letter To The Editor
of *Inside The Vatican*

by Dr. Rosalie A. Turton
November 12, 1996

*(This letter was addressed to Mr. Robert Moynihan,
Editor of Inside the Vatican, and appeared
in the Dec., 1996 issue of that magazine.)*

As Director of the 101 Foundation, the Akita center of the United States, may I bring to your attention a common error which was reiterated by Ms. Daniele Palmieri in her fine article on Our Lady of Akita, in the October, 1996 issue of *Inside The Vatican.*

It was rumored that on July 26, 1973, the face, hands, neck, and feet of the statue of Our Lady of Akita shed blood. This was not the case, since only the right hand of the statue shed blood. In order to correct this erroneous but widely circulated statement, Bishop John Shojiro Ito, Ordinary of Niigata, the diocese in which Akita is located, subsequently issued a letter to interested parties and Akita centers throughout the world, clarifying the matter.

Ms. Palmieri also suggested that this statue "seems to be the only one in the world directly connected to a cross—the cross is carved out of the same block of wood as the statue and is connected to Mary's back from the heart downward." She intimated that many believe that therein lies a profound connection between Mary's maternal suffering and the suffering of Jesus, her Son, indicating Mary's implied role as Co-Redemptrix.

That is indeed true, but it should be pointed out there are at least two other important images which are similarly connected to the cross. The first one is Our Lady of All Peoples (commonly known as Our Lady of All Nations), the cult of which has been recently approved by Monsignor Henry Bommers, the Bishop of Haarlem, Holland, on May 31, 1996. It was actually from a picture of his image that Our Lady of Akita was hand carved in Japan, by Buddhist sculptor, Mr. Saburo Wakasa. The visionary in Amsterdam, Holland, was Ms. Ida Peerdeman, and Our Lady indicated there that she was our Co-Redemptrix, Mediatrix, and Advocate.

The second image that is becoming widely known is Our Lady of the Cross. This image was shown in a vision to Mr. Carver Alan Ames of Perth, Australia, who has a positive endorsement of his Archbishop, the Most Reverend Barry J. Hickey.

Dr. Mark Miravalle, founder of Vox Populi Mariae Mediatrici, stated that nearly 4 million petitions to establish as Dogma, Mary as our Co-Redemptrix, Mediatrix, and Advocate have been sent to the Holy Father. Our Lady told Ida Peerdeman that this will, indeed, occur, and it will take place on May 31. The year is not known, but with the great fervor and momentum which is currently being aroused, many believe that it will be very soon.

Our Lady of Akita

Our Lady of All Nations
(also known as Our Lady of All Peoples)

Our Lady of Garabandal
(also known as Our Lady of Mt. Carmel)

Above and below: Our Lady of Mt. Carmel

*Above: Painting of a vision given to C. Alan Ames of
Mary, Queen of the Cross*

Messages About The Vision Of Mary, Queen Of The Cross

Our Lady—12/31/94

Red is the color of my Son's blood which was shed for mankind, red is the color of His love. As I stood by the cross I shared in my Son's suffering and pain, I shared in His love. White is the color of the water that flowed from His side, the water that washes man's sins away in love. As I stood by the cross I shared in the giving of this water.

Gold is the color of the cross, the cross of the King. Gold on my garment shows that I was with my Son on the cross.

The smile of love shows the deep love I have for my children...a mother's love.

The Scapular shows mankind that my love can be attained by wearing my sign.

The Rosary tells my children to pray and pray the Rosary. It is through prayer that I lead you to Jesus.

My outstretched hand is there for my children to take so that I can walk with them to my Son Jesus.

My arms are opened to embrace my children in an eternal joining of our hearts to become one in Jesus.

I ask to be called "Queen of the Cross," because the Father has granted me the grace of sharing in the redemption of mankind with my Son Jesus who by His sacrifice has opened the door of Heaven to His children.

Jesus—1/16/95 (About Queen of the Cross painting)

A painting of love, a painting of Mother.
A painting of giving, a painting of Mother.
A painting of offering, a painting of Mother.
A painting from Heaven, a painting of Mother.
A painting from God, a painting of Mother.
A painting from sanctity, a painting of Mother.
A painting for all, a painting of Mother.

Our Lady—1/16/95

Nailed to the cross was my Son Jesus, pain filled His body and soul. As I watched, an agony within burned so deeply I could not stand. On my knees I prayed and prayed, on my knees I wept for my Son's agony to end, and on my knees I saw the glory of God. I saw how much God loves His children, how much He was prepared to give to save them and how much He needed to forgive them. Nailed to the cross with my Son was my spirit, my being, my self. Nailed to the cross with my Son was my love, not as an equal but as a handmaiden wanting to serve her Lord and her God. In the service of Jesus was I, as I watched His supreme act of love, a service I long all to share with me so they can find the rewards that await them in Heaven, the rewards of God.

Our Lady—1/17/95

Queen of the Cross, Queen of Sorrow, Queen of Heaven. The cross and the sorrow show the way to Heaven and I as Queen lead to God.

Our Lady—12/4/94

By the cross I stood and watched my Son Jesus give His life for man. I stood and prayed to the Father in Heaven to forgive them for what they did. I prayed to the Father to ease the pain of Jesus and I prayed for strength to see Jesus through this terrible suffering. With John at my side, we offered all our love to the Father if He would ease the suffering just a little. We offered all of ourselves if He would lift this burden from the Messiah. I knew He could not, for this sacrifice was needed to release man from his own chains, the chains that mankind had brought upon himself. 1 wanted to embrace my Son and comfort Him; I wanted to hold Him in my arms and tell Him I loved Him and His mother was there; I wanted to smother Him with affection as I did when He was a child.

I wanted my Son to live but I knew He could not, that He must endure death so that He could show how much God loves man. The tears of sorrow that ran from my eyes created pools of love, pools of motherly care, and pools of everlasting joy. The heaviness of my heart created the love that I have for all mankind, created the special bond between myself and all of mankind.

Now I shed tears again as my foolish children follow the path of self destruction, follow the path of evil and sin. Do I have to have my heart broken again? Do I have to endure the sorrow that comes when a mother sees her children hurt themselves? Do I have to mourn again at the death of my children, a death that will last forever?

All I want for my children is goodness, all I want for my children is love, all I want for my children is Heaven. I want all for my children. If mankind can change now, if mankind can start to pray, to love God and each other, receive the sacraments often and live the life that God created them for, then and only then can this planet become the paradise it was meant to be. If mankind can learn to forgive, to accept others regardless of differences and become one family, the family of God, then and only then can eternity be theirs (in Heaven).

Prayer for Graces:
"If these prayers are said when holding
my picture as Queen of the Cross
on your heart, the person praying
will be given a grace from God."

I ask the Lord to grant me, through His Blessed Mother Mary, Queen of the Cross, this grace (mention what you are praying for). Say:

Three Hail Mary's
Three Our Father's, and
Three Glory Be's

Introduction

by Carver Alan Ames

I was baptized a Catholic but as I grew up I did not believe. I thought the Catholic faith was like a fairy story, it was not true; just fiction.

I never prayed much...maybe a minute at night as an insurance policy that if I died, God would take me to Heaven. The times I went to church were usually Christmas and Easter, just to keep the faith, in case it was true. During my early years I would steal from the offering boxes in the church, because we didn't have much money, due to an alcoholic gambling father. I only stopped this when I was caught by the police. I joined a motorcycle gang and became very violent and a drunkard. Then I met my wife Kathryn who quieted me down a little. After a while though, I fell back into my old ways of violence, alcohol, stealing, and so much more. My life was a life of almost completely turning away from God.

One day when many bad things were happening in my life and I wondered what was to become of me, a sweet voice started talking to me from out of nowhere. I thought I was going mad and that maybe the alcohol might have caused this to happen. The voice said she was an angel and that God had sent her to me because He loved me and wanted my love. I was unsure that she was real, so I asked her to prove that she was, and so she did. She told me of things that would happen in my life, all of which did occur. This convinced me it was true.

A few months later St. Teresa of Avila started talking to me, and in no uncertain terms told me to change my life or I would spend an eternity in suffering. St. Teresa asked me to pray the Rosary three times a day, which for a man like me seemed impossible. With her help I started to pray the Rosary and didn't want to stop. That was certainly a miracle in my life. Another miracle was that I stopped drinking, and for someone who was nearly an alcoholic, it was a wonderful grace. As time went on, other saints spoke to me, encouraging me to pray and to receive the sacraments.

One day when I was in front of a Sacred Heart Statue, it started to shine white. All of a sudden I could see Our Blessed Mother Mary...so beautiful, so peaceful. I was a little confused because I could see her Heart which I thought was the Heart from the Statue behind. It was only later that I discovered I was seeing the Immaculate Heart of Mary. I had never heard of it before.

Our Blessed Mother told me she loved me and I should call her Mother (now I often call her Mom), as she truly is everyone's Mother. She explained that she wanted to take me, through prayer and the sacraments, deeper into the Heart of Jesus, and that this is what she offers all mankind. Our Blessed Mother continues to talk and sometimes appear to me, always encouraging me to pray, to receive the sacraments, and to trust in God. During one discussion Mother Mary said to me, "My Son is coming to you," and then Jesus, Our Lord was there.

My Mini Judgment

One day in February, 1994, the most wonderful thing happened. Jesus spoke to me. Jesus told me that He loved me and that I should love myself. Jesus then took me through my life; I saw all the sins I had committed, all the pain I had caused.

Jesus showed me how I had hurt Him. I saw Jesus on the cross suffering and I knew my sins had contributed to it. I also saw how I had hurt others and how I hurt myself.

Later I was shown the state of my soul. It was dark, covered with what appeared to be sores which erupted with foul smelling pus. I was told this was my soul in sin. Then I was shown how my soul could be so bright, so clean, so pure. Jesus said He would forgive me if I asked for it, and so I did. I felt so badly for what I had done to Jesus and seeing His suffering on the cross, I cried for hours.

Jesus also took me through all the hurtful times I had, all the feelings of being unloved, unwanted, unworthy. Jesus told me He always loved me and He always would. He told me I had been forgiven, and that now I had to love and forgive myself. It was very difficult to do, but with Jesus' help, I finally managed to do it.

The whole experience lasted all afternoon (approximately 5 hours) most of which I spent crying on the bed and asking Jesus to forgive me. I knew I could never sin again as it hurt Jesus. At that time I fell in love with Him and promised that I would do all that He asked of me, willingly and without conditions. That day I truly returned to God.

As I said, Jesus told me He loved me and He wanted to forgive me my sins. I asked, "Why me?" Why did God, His Mother, angels and saints come to me, a sinner, instead of a good person? Jesus said "I love you the same as everyone else. The only difference is how much you love me. If I can change someone like you, who is so far away from Me, it shows mankind it does not matter who you are or what you have done, I love you and I want to forgive you, if only you ask for it. This will show that God is here for all mankind, not just for a select few!"

I fell in love with Jesus on that day, and now I love him every second of every day. Jesus asked me, a sinner, if I would do His work. I felt so unworthy, not the right person to do this, but Jesus said that I was worthy and that by dedicating my life to Him, I would show how much I loved Him. I agreed to do His Will, and have promised that, no matter what God asks of me, I will do it because I love Him.

God, His Mother, the angels and saints started to give me messages for mankind, and asked me to publish them in a book. With limited funds, we published two small booklets, "The Way" and "The Obvious Way." Now with the help of so many good people, we have combined these two, plus another booklet, "The Way of Life" into this one book.

I hope those who read this book see God's love in every word, a love He wants all to share, and a love that brings you to eternal Joy. May God bless you all. I thank you for reading this book. It is a great reward for me, a sinner, who loves God. Please pray for me, your servant in the love of Jesus and Mary.

Part I
The Way To God

Chapters: Page:

1. The Way to God—   1.
   Messages from Our Lady
2. The Way with God—   29.
   Messages from God, The Father
3. The Way of God's Mercy—   38.
   Messages from God, The Holy Spirit
4. The Way to Eternal Love—   46.
   Messages from God, The Son

Part II
The Obvious Way

1. The Sins of Mankind—   53.
   Messages from God, The Father
2. Under the Name of Reason—   67.
   Messages from Our Lady
3. Misunderstanding The Way—   70.
   Messages from God, The Father
4. The Way Home—   80.
   Messages from God, The Holy Trinity

Part III
The Way Of Life

1. The People—   138.
   Messages from God, The Son
2. The Sacraments—   157.
   Messages from God, The Son
3. The Church—   163.
   Messages from God, The Son
4. The Advice—   166.
   Messages from God, The Holy Trinity
   and from Our Lady

I offer this book to the
Mother of Majesty
who gave me these words.

Chapter 1.

The Way to God—
Messages from Our Lady

Our Lady—8/26/94

Man has taken a long time to come to the decision that there may not be a God, but then again there may be. Man sits on the fence and makes no profession of faith. He just waits to see what happens before he commits himself.

How can man call himself a free thinker if he cannot make a free choice to say, "Yes, there is a God," or "No, there is not." Some of those who profess to believe in God only believe with doubts and reservations, only accept God's existence, God's word if it suits them. If it is something too difficult they ignore or deny God. Those who do not believe in God, do not believe until they need God and then hope there is a God.

Now man thinks with his reason and his science. He uses these to try to discover the truth of creation and the truth of God. Now man thinks as if he is God, as if he is the ruler and owner of all. Now man thinks that if he can unlock the secrets of the universe, he will be the equal of Him who created all things.

To understand God's creations is not the answer to all. To understand where they came from and how they exist is not the answer to the great mystery of God. The great mystery can never be solved by man. He can never comprehend the mystery, the majesty, the greatness, the divinity of God.

One day man unlocks the door to a perplexing question only to find another, more difficult one awaiting. One day man will unlock the door to creation, only to find it is the wrong door and find more questions to be answered than he started with.

If only man could see with eyes of faith, all would be so simple. In the eyes of faith all answers are easily found and all questions just fade away.

Man is here by God's grace. God gave man life and gave man reason. God supplied all that man needs to exist in happiness. God gave man all that man needed to lead fulfilled lives. God gave man all.

If man cannot see this, then it is time for him to stop and look closely at himself and see what his disbelief in God and God's gifts has cost him. Man has only to look back in time. For as long as there are written words of the past man has been in trouble. Wars, murder, stealing, hatred, greed, starvation, pestilence, lust, immorality abound throughout history and yet man follows the same path over and over again. Does not man learn from past mistakes? Look back and see when was there peace and happiness? There never was, not since man first sinned.

If sinning has only brought death, destruction, pain and sorrow, why keep to it? Why do over and over what has failed in the past? If something is unsuccessful, then surely a new strategy should be tried.

The old ways have failed. Why not try a new way and maybe a new age will arrive? The new way is as old as time but it has never been embraced by man. It is the way of God. The way of love. The way of kindness. The way of softness. The way of gentleness. The way of Jesus.

Jesus brought the old word of God, His Father, alive. He was that Word. Jesus showed man how God's words should be used. Used as God meant them to be, not man. Jesus showed that if we all lived to God's word, the world would become the paradise that it was supposed to be. Jesus showed the way. Now is the time for man to try to follow it.

What can you do to follow it? It is easy, LOVE. Live in love of God, love of fellow man, and love of yourself. Treat everyone and everything as a gift from God. See God's spark in all things and treat them accordingly. Treat them with love.

This is a hard path to follow, but if you make the effort then maybe your efforts will help save the world and mankind from themselves.

What a task man has made for himself to discover by science and reason who is God, what is God, and where is God.

How can science and reason answer this? Only faith can. Science and reason cannot unravel what is impossible to know, only faith can understand it. Science and reason cannot understand what is outside science and reason, only faith can.

Could science and reason cure many incurable diseases?

No, only faith can.

Can science and reason bring manna from heaven?

No, only faith can.

Does science and reason show man the reality of life and living?

No, only faith can.

What then can science and reason do? They can only do what man lets them do. It could do a lot more with faith in God, for God is the great scientist, the great reckoner. God's reason is sound, unlike man's. God's reason is pure, unlike man's. God's reason is love, unlike man's.

What is the good of science and reason if they lead you nowhere or only to pain and suffering? This is what most of man's science and reason does.

Why cannot man just say, "Lord, show me the way," and God will. He will show man the best way for man. He will show man the easiest way for man, and He will show man the most loving way for man to be.

When time began was man there? When all was created was man there? When life was made, was man there? No, only God was. So, if God was, is, and always will be, why does not man turn to Him and ask Him? If you ask Him, He will answer you.

Man, even though he does not know it, lives in faith in God. Faith that there will be air to breathe, faith that the sun will shine, faith that the earth will still exist, faith that his life will go on, faith that his whole existence remains, and faith that his time is still to come. So much faith in God, but man cannot see this. He has been blinded by science and reason. When science and reason are misused, it is just another name for sin.

Like all of creation, God loves man. Like all of creation, God made man. Like all of creation, man is God's. When man comes to understand and believe this, he will finally realize his true destiny in God.

When man accepts who created him, who man is, what he was created for, then man can come to live in love and happiness.

When man accepts Jesus as his Savior and Lord, his champion against evil, his love, his way to the Father in Heaven, then man will start to know his future, his way to live, his way to love, and his way to be.

Jesus must be accepted by all mankind as Lord. Jesus must be accepted by all mankind as risen from the dead. Jesus must be accepted by all mankind as the true Son of God who with the Holy Spirit, is one with the Father.

When mankind learns this and accepts it in faith, then the world can become the paradise it was supposed to be. When mankind learns this, the world will finally live in peace, harmony and love.

Most of the world wants to live this way, so why does it not happen? Most of the world wants peace, love, and security. Most of the world looks for this, but cannot find it because it looks in the wrong places.

If only the world would look to the Lord God Jesus' words, actions, and prayers, it would see that this is the true way to peace. Is not the Lord Jesus the Prince of Peace? Is not the Lord Jesus the living love of God? Is not the Lord Jesus the only true security for man?

What is man looking for today? Man is looking for himself, when man should be looking for God. God is watching and waiting to help. God is watching and longing to help. God is watching and longing to have His love accepted.

When man does this, his complete self will change into the being he should be. What good has looking to, trusting, and believing in man done? Now, turn to God, trust, believe, and love in and through God and find the true happiness man strives for.

Our Lady—8/26/94

PRAYER

What is prayer? Prayer is talking with God. Prayer is a conversation with God. Prayer is a communication with God.

If prayer is used properly, it can bring everything to mankind—peace, prosperity, love, happiness, and joy. It can bring God to man. It can bring all.

When you talk to close friends, loved ones, you open your heart to them. This is how prayer should be, for God is your friend, your love, your all. When you talk to friends and loved ones you listen to what they say to you. This is how prayer should be, not only talking but listening, listening to God. When you pray, if you listen, God answers in many ways. God answers with love.

Prayers are a special time when God sits with you and listens to what you say. He listens and loves. He only waits for you to offer your prayers to Him so that He can answer them.

When you ask in prayer and humility, love and truth, God answers you. He may not answer in the way you want or expect, but He answers in the way which is best for your soul. He sees how you really need to be answered and He answers.

Prayer should be an uplifting experience. It is not uplifting when it becomes a chore or duty. Prayer should be spontaneous love and it should be a complete abandonment of yourself.

Prayer is the charge that re-ignites your soul with God's love and light. Prayer is such a special gift from God that it should be cherished. Prayer is for your higher self, your soul. Prayer is for your good and the good of others. Prayer is a special grace from God to mankind. Prayer is a time of joy for God because His children come to Him in love.

Prayer is glorifying yourself and your God. Prayer is for all.

Prayer can be any words not just those taught to you. Apart from the Lord's Prayer, God likes nothing more than to hear your own words, your own feelings, your own thoughts.

Prayer is not only words. You also pray in your actions. If you wish to show God's love to others or glorify God by your actions, then this is also prayer. This is how you can pray continuously, by your actions.

The prayer of silence, when you just sit quietly with the Lord, can be the most rewarding time. This can be when the Lord speaks to you by words, feelings, thoughts, or pictures. This can be the most beautiful time of all, knowing the Lord is talking to you.

This prayer of silence needs to be an uninterrupted time. Sit in a quiet room, put up a "Do not disturb" sign, unhook the telephone, allow no distractions, just sit and say, "Lord, this time is Yours. Help me to listen to Your word, help me be in You, help me be with You." Then just sit relaxed and try to think of one word over and over. The most special word ever, the most giving word ever, the most loving word ever, the most glorious word ever. What word?

Why, "Jesus" of course. If you keep saying in your mind, "Jesus, Jesus, Jesus," you will start to see and feel God's message coming to you.

There will be many distractions. Your mind will wander, strange thoughts will try to take you away—thoughts of family, of work, of sports, of anything, will come. Just keep saying "Jesus, Jesus" and all this will go and you will come to the glory of God. It may take some time, more than one or two attempts may be needed, but persevere, then set a time every day and enjoy being with God.

Here are some prayers to say in normal prayer time...

My Father in heaven, I love You and I ask for the forgiveness of my sins.

My Father in heaven, I love You and I ask You to listen to my words of love for You.

My Father in heaven, I love You and I ask for Your love.

My Lord Jesus, my Savior, my Redeemer, my Love, take me by the hand and lead me to Your Father in heaven.

My Lord Jesus, my Savior, my Redeemer, my Love, take me by the hand and lead me to Your glory in heaven.

My Lord Jesus, my Savior, my Redeemer, my Love, take me by the hand and lead me to Your special place You have made for me in heaven.

Holy Spirit of God, the Fire, the Dove, the Wind, and the light of God, fill me with Thee.

Fill me with Thy fire, Thy peace, Thy words, and Thy love.

Holy Spirit of God, set me free in Thee.

Holy Spirit of God, light me up with God's graces.

Sweet Mother of God, Queen of Heaven, listen to my prayers and ask your Son, your Spouse, and your Father to answer me.

Sweet Saints of God, with the graces God has given you, I implore you to represent me to God and to ask the Lord to answer my prayers.

Angels of God, I ask you to watch over me and protect me so that I may serve the Lord and come to Him on my final day.

O Holy Trinity, O Holy God, O Holy One, I adore Thee, I worship Thee, I praise Thee, I thank Thee, and I love Thee.

Sweet Lord, love me.

ttt

Our Lady—8/26/94

DEVOTION

Devotion is especially important in your love of God. Those who devote themselves to God's work and love, receive special rewards and gifts from the Lord.

Those who offer to do all for God regardless, those who do all for God regardless, already have a special gift from God. There are many more gifts He wishes to give and often does give.

The only thing that stops God giving gifts is the person himself. Sometimes they are so busy doing God's work they forget God. They forget to spend time alone with God. They forget to pray and often they forget the sacraments.

To devote yourself to God, first and foremost means you must keep in His love through prayers and sacraments. If you forget to do this, you may end up doing your own work, not God's. You may do the opposite of what God wants. You may even get trapped by the dark and be unaware of it. So, always pray and always receive the sacraments.

The sacraments strengthen you in God, they fill you with God, they purify you.

††

Our Lady—8/27/94

ADORATION

Adoration is reserved for One alone. Adoration is for the glory of only One. Adoration can only be given to God.

Adoration is for the Lord Jesus. Adoration is for the Holy Spirit and adoration is for the Father in heaven. Adoration is for the One, True God who is Three. Adoration is for the Holy Trinity. Adoration is for God only.

When you adore God, you show Him your love. When you adore God, you show others that you love Him. When you adore God, you show your faith in Him.

Adoration is a special gift you give to God, a gift which He first gave to you and now you return this gift.

Adoration is an act of humility when you proclaim the Lord above all others and bow down before Him as His humble servant.

Finally, adoration is a complete giving of yourself to God in love, a complete acknowledgment that you are here by God's grace and love. It is the only act you can do by your own choice, for once you adore God everything else follows naturally. It is making this choice that opens you to God.

It is only when you adore God that you completely surrender to His love, to Him.

Our Lady—8/27/94

VENERATION

To venerate is not to adore or worship. To venerate is to praise and thank the angels, the saints, and the most Holy Mother of God for their sacrifices, for their giving, for their help, and for their love.

To venerate Our Lady Mother of God is a very special veneration. The Mother of God has received unique graces from God, unique gifts, and a unique position. With her giving of herself completely to God to bring His Son into the world and to nurture and love Him until He achieved manhood, then to be with Him as He gave His life for man to God, and finally to be taken into Heaven by the Lord without a blemish on her soul...what a special spirit. Crowned Queen of Heaven, Immaculate Heart, Mother of God, Mother of Man, Mother of All Nations, Mother of Majesty, Mother of Mercy, Daughter of God, Spouse of God, what a joyous spirit this is, Mary Mother in Heaven.

When you venerate Our Lady, she has special graces that God has given her to help man overcome sin and come to God. She has been given the task of loving man, helping man, and with the Lord Jesus at her side, defeating evil in the final day.

It is wonderful to venerate the Mother of God and to pray to her for her help, love, and compassion, but it is important to remember that Our Lady always leads to the Lord Jesus, the Holy Spirit, and the Father. She is not God's equal, but God's servant. This must always be kept in mind.

The veneration of saints brings God great pleasure because He can grant gifts through His beloved ones to His children.

This is a special reward to the saints for the sacrifices which they have made for God. This is a great gift that each saint treasures. This is a wonderful love from God.

The saints always lead to God through His Son Jesus. The saints are the servants of Jesus who have given their all for Him. The saints are what mankind should try to be.

Our Lady—8/27/94

LIVING WITH GOD

Living with God is what we do all the time whether or not we know it or believe it. God made all things, therefore everything is from God including us, so we must be living and using the creations of God at all times.

The electricity you use daily comes from God. It is a creation of His to help man live and advance in love. Electricity is an invisible force that can move objects, faith is like that.

Faith is more powerful than any other force that God has given man. With faith anything is possible, seas can be parted, mountains moved, illness cured, and souls saved.

Faith is the most important gift that man has, but he does not use it as he should.

If you can believe that electricity is there and it will power your light in your house when you switch it on, then you should believe that faith will power your soul when you switch it on.

You believe in electricity because you can see the results when you flick the switch. Faith is the same. You can see the results when you flick the switch of faith in God. How many miracles have occurred because of faith in God? Yet many still do not believe. They see these acts as unusual, special only for a few. Miracles should be everyday events, happening everywhere, if only man had faith in God.

When man can come to terms with the fact that he only exists by God's grace, then man can truly start to live as he was supposed to.

When man understands that love is the key to living with and in God, then man can become the true being that he was created to be.

When mankind accepts that the Lord Jesus is love and that to follow His way is to follow God, then mankind will become the shining light he was meant to be.

When mankind lives in love, not hate, helps each other, does not take advantage of others; when mankind becomes compassionate, loving, joyful in God, then, and only then, can mankind receive the place that is reserved for him in heaven.

Man must now look to helping himself as a species, as brothers and sisters in God. Regardless of race or color, wealth or poverty, fame or obscurity, to God, all are equal. The only way to heaven is through the Lord Jesus in love, hope, faith, goodness, kindness, and truth. It does not matter what you have or who you are on earth, all that matters is how you live. Do you live in the love of God or in the love of yourself? Do you help others or help yourself? Do you want others to prosper or only yourself?

What does man need to live? What does man need to exist? What does man need to be? Man only needs God, for God is everything.

What does man need to have around him? What does man need within him? What does man need to feed him? Only God, for God is everything.

What does man want to be? What does man strive for? What does man desire? Whatever it is, he will find it in God.

What does man look for in life? What does man look for in others? What does man look for in himself? Whatever it is, he will find it in God.

Man is lost without God. Man is a simple soul who needs God for everything. Man is a product of God's love. Man is a wish for the future, a wish for love, peace, warmth, friendship. If man can put on these garments, he can become the true child of God. If man can open himself to God, he can become the true creation God wanted him to be and if man can address his sins, he can become pure in God.

Man has to learn how to love. Man has to learn how to live. Man has to learn how to help each other and, most of all, man has to learn how to love God. If man learns, then pain, suffering, hunger, hate, greed, envy, and all the things of the dark will fade away. A new light will shine in man, the light of Jesus, the light of God.

✝✝✝

Our Lady—8/27/94

PROCLAIMING GOD TO THE WORLD

Many people love God, but love Him in a private and personal way. When it comes to talking to others about this love, many get embarrassed or uncomfortable. Why is this? Is it because you do not want others to know you truly believe or is it because you are afraid that others will ridicule you?

If you do not want others to know, this stems from fear: fear of ridicule, fear of being on the outside of the group, fear of others, so really there is only one reason, fear.

Fear is what stops you proclaiming God to the world. This fear is a human emotion that can be overcome with the Lord's help. Just ask Him and He will lift this fear from you.

Once you see it does not matter what others say or do to you and it only matters how God sees you, this fear will disappear. When you lift this fear with God's help, you will find your whole life changes. You will be happy to shout the Lord's praises to the world. You will be happy to proclaim Jesus as Lord to the world and you will just be happy.

True happiness only comes from God. True happiness is a gift from God. True happiness is there for you if you want it. Just proclaim the Lord God Jesus to the world and it will be yours.

Our Lady—8/27/94

SHOWING THE WORLD GOD'S LOVE

How do you show the world you love God and you want to share it with everyone you meet?

You show it by being kind and generous to others, by helping others when possible, by putting others before yourself, by perfecting the art of giving yourself and your time, by becoming living love. Most importantly though, is praising God to others in the good things you do.

When you give yourself, you must always remind yourself and others why you are giving, you are giving for God. God gave the supreme sacrifice when, through His Son Jesus, He gave His life for man. You must always remind all that your giving pales in comparison. It is but a minuscule act in comparison to God's sacrifice. The difference is so great that even if you were to give your life for others, it still is not even the same as one word the Lord spoke.

If you recall that the Lord saved you by His sacrifice, then your giving should become easier, more complete, and more rewarding. Never forget to show how you wish to repay God, if only a little, for saving you.

At all times proclaim how great is God's love, and how it is this that makes you want to give love freely to all.

ttt

Our Lady—8/27/94

WORSHIPPING THE LORD

Worshipping the Lord is shown by your praise of the Lord, your actions in the Lord and your deeds for the Lord.

Your praise of the Lord is through your prayers and through your talks with God. You should not only praise God for all the good things that have happened to you, but also the disappointments and losses you may have had. What is praise of the Lord if you only praise Him when you are happy? Anyone can praise in happy times. It is when you praise in sad times, that you show your true love of God. Thank God and praise God always, no matter what the situation is. This is truly the praise and thanks that God treasures most. If you do this, you will also find that in difficult times your burdens seem lighter and in good times they seem better.

Your actions and deeds for the Lord God are also a way of worshipping God. Every time you start a day just say, "I offer everything I do today in worship of the Lord." Then try to show your love in everything you do, no matter how hard it may be. In very difficult or trying times, show your love and show it more and offer it in worship to God. This is true worship of the Lord.

Our Lady—8/27/94

ATONING FOR THE SINS OF OTHERS

Atoning for the sins of others is a very important part of the love of God. If, by your prayers, you can save but one soul, you bring great joy to heaven.

Each day when you pray to the Lord it is important that you pray for others, living and dead. If, by your prayers, you make the difference that may bring a living person, a lost soul to God, then it is surely your duty to pray for them.

When you pray for people, it is important to pray for what is best for their soul and not what is best for their pocket. It is, of course, good to pray for food for the hungry, relief of pain for the suffering, freedom for the oppressed, and rights for those who have none. What are these though if their soul is not saved? You should pray for their souls' needs first and their bodies' needs second. This may be difficult for some people to understand, but try to imagine this. If you were in a desert and dying of thirst and you were offered water that would save you until tomorrow, or you were offered spirit filled drink that would sustain you until you reached safety, which would you take? Of course, the spirit filled drink! So it is with your prayers. You must pray for what will sustain the soul so that it can come to God's glory in heaven.

In your prayers for lost souls, whom are you praying for? You are praying for those who do not know God, for those who do not believe in God, and for those who believe in other so-called gods.

By your prayers you may open a soul to understand, to believe, to accept, to love God. What a victory this is for God, for a lost sheep that returns is very special to the Lord. So always include these in your prayers, and ask that the Holy Spirit will come upon them.

When you pray for the dead, whom are you praying for? There are two types of souls you must pray for.

There are those in purgatory who are repenting for their sins and are away from God until they have repaid their mistakes on earth. They will eventually see God, so God gives you a grace that if you pray for these souls, He will lift them from purgatory.

The other souls you should pray for are those who are on their way to hell. If you ask in your prayers for the Lord God to save them and to take them to purgatory instead, how can He not listen, for He is a God of love? If you knew the suffering in hell, you would not wish anyone, no matter what they have done, to go there. Surely also, if you love God, then you can forgive even the worst sinner, for this is what Jesus did with His sacrifice at Calvary.

Our Lady—8/27/94

PRAYING FOR THE HOLY SPIRIT
TO FILL YOU

It is important that all persons asks the Holy Spirit to come upon them. Did not the Lord Jesus say, "I will send My Spirit, the Paraclete, upon you?" If Jesus has said this, then it is our duty as His followers, as Christians, to ask for the Holy Spirit to fill us with God's fire and love.

How can we do this? The first and most important thing is to open yourself completely to the Lord. Do not say this or that cannot be done, or this cannot happen to me. All is possible with God. How many times did Jesus show that nothing is beyond the love of God?

Next, you must completely adore the Lord and proclaim Him as your Lord and Master, your God. Tell God you love Him and that you are an empty vessel waiting for Him to use. Then ask the Holy Spirit to fill you with God's love and light, to break you free from the chains that bind you to earth. The chains of self and of sin. Promise the Lord you will not sin again with His help and ask the Lord to forgive all your sins. Then on your knees before God, you could say these words:-

My Lord God Jesus Christ, I am Yours.

My Lord God Jesus Christ, You promised Your children Your spirit would come upon us. I ask now humbly that Your Holy Spirit touches my soul and brings me to You, Your Father, and Your Spirit. Amen.

ttt

Our Lady—8/27/94

PRAYERS FOR FORGIVENESS

I ask the Lord God Jesus Christ to forgive my sins. I ask with the knowledge that I live in a state of sin and it is only the Lord who can forgive me. Amen.

Forgive me Lord, for I have sinned.

I ask for Your mercy, I ask for Your love, and I ask for You to help me not sin again. Amen.

Please Lord, lift the stain of sin from my soul, lift the pain of offending You from me, and lift me up to You in glory. Amen.

My sins are so great, my sins are so dark, my sins are so painful when I think of how they hurt You Lord Jesus.

Please forgive me and teach me how not to sin again. Amen.

On the cross You forgave me, on the cross You redeemed me, and on the cross You saved me. Now I humbly ask You to help me to become what You want me to be.

I ask forgiveness, Your help, and Your love sweet Jesus. Amen.

ttt

Our Lady—8/27/94

THE HOLY TRINITY

Many people find it difficult to understand the Holy Trinity—how can one being be three? It all comes to faith, faith that with God all is possible.

God has given these words to help explain:

The Holy Trinity is Me and I am They. I am the Father, the Son, and the Holy Spirit. I am God, We are God.

What a wondrous thing, three in one and one in three. Each God, each different, each the same, each, one with Me.

All came from Me, all is Me, all is God.

The Father the Creator, the Son the love, the Spirit the fire.

Together God, separate God, together the creator, together the love, together the fire.

One being, one God, three aspects, three different reflections of God.

What a mystery, what divine love, what heavenly glory, what joy!

Our Lady—8/27/94

HOW TO FILL YOURSELF WITH LOVE

How to fill yourself with love is a question that all followers of Jesus the Lord ask at some time in their journey to God.

Most people find it easy to love those that they find likeable, appealing, or friendly. When it comes to people you find hard to like, to love, to even talk to, then this is when you show God you truly are His.

It must be the same for all people, regardless of race, color, creed. You must love everyone the same. This is hard to do, often because you put your own considerations first. You put what you think into your love for others not what God asks. God asks you to love all, not just those who fit into your own personal requirements and needs.

If you consider that God, through His Son Jesus, put a spark of Himself within every human and that God who created us created us equally, then how can we deny anyone love?

When you look at others, remember that God is in everyone and everyone is from God, we are all His sons and daughters, then you may find it easier in those difficult moments. Try to see Jesus in everyone and then try to treat them the way you would treat the Lord if He were standing before you. If you can try to love everyone, then you will find one day you are so full of love, that nothing is too difficult.

Tägliche Übung ab dem 27. 5. 02 - 24. 32 Uhr !

Our Lady—8/27/94

PRAYERS FOR LOVE

Sweetest Lord Jesus, You love all mankind the same. In Your mercy, teach me to love all as You do. Amen.

Lord Jesus, Lord of Love, Love, complete Love. Show me Your love, so that through me Your love can be shown to the world. Amen.

Love of God, Love of Man, Love of All. Sweet Jesus, this is what I pray for. Amen.

Fill me with Your love, Lord Jesus.

Fill me with Your compassion, Lord Jesus.

Fill me with You, so that I can love others.

Lord, You showed Your love on the cross.

Lord, You shed Your blood for love.

Lord, You gave Your life for love.

Now Lord, I ask You to show me how to give my love. Amen.

Our Lady—8/27/94

TAKING THE SPIRIT OF GOD TO OTHERS

To bring the Spirit of God to others is the duty of all who follow Jesus, for Jesus said His Spirit was for all mankind, not just a chosen few. His Spirit was for all who proclaim the Holy Trinity as the one true God.

The way to take the Spirit of God to others is through love and love alone. The love you show others you have for your God, the love you show others you have for them, and the love you show others that you have for all.

You show your love by helping them understand God through His Son Jesus. For what greater love can you show, than to give them the way to eternal happiness in God.

You can bring the Spirit of God to others by the words of the Lord in the Bible.

Most of all you can bring the Spirit of God to others by your example of living your life in God's Commandments.

Even if others all around you live in sin knowingly or unknowingly, by your living to the commandments of the Lord, others see God's Spirit in you. When they see your kindness, love, goodness, friendliness, they say, "What a nice person. I wish I could be like that." This is the beginning, the opening, that will let the Spirit touch their soul.

✝✝✝

Our Lady—8/27/94

THE WAY TO TRUE HAPPINESS

Everyone, no matter who they are, longs for true happiness. Even with all the wealth and fame, all the intelligence, all the friends, and with all the status, man still longs for more. Man is not happy no matter what earthly things he has.

He always looks for more: more money, fame, answers, friends, status...there is never enough, so man is never truly happy. More, more, more is the way that man thinks he will find happiness.

In fact, the reverse is true. Less, less, less is the way.

Think less of yourself and more of God.

Think less of yourself and more of others and think less of yourself and more of your environment.

The less you think of yourself, the more God thinks of you.

The less you have now, the more your rewards in heaven will be.

The less you need now, the more you will receive in gifts from God.

True happiness can only be found in God. When you are in love with God, nothing more is required. Nothing more is needed. You look no further, for God is all.

Happiness is God, and God is happiness.

†††

Our Lady—10/24/94

Unsure of love, unsure of happiness, unsure of God. Unsure is man of love, unsure is man of wanting happiness, unsure is man of God's existence. Only man is unsure, only man is unfaithful, only man is blind. Man must become sure in faith and open his eyes to God's love and happiness. What a joy man will find awaiting him if he takes faith, love, and God by the hand.

†††

Our Lady—10/24/94

These are the messages God wants you to give with your first steps:

The Eucharist is the body and blood of Jesus; when taken within, it sets fire to the soul of the receiver with love. It is only the receiver who stops this by disbelief or by lack of faith. The Eucharist should be received often, daily.

Confession should be received often, at least monthly, but weekly is much better. To receive forgiveness from God is special and should be sought more often.

Love everyone as you love yourself.

Love God and show this by your actions to others and by your devotion to Jesus.

These are the ways to true happiness.

Our Lady—10/25/94

I look down on the world filled with sorrow, filled with pain, filled with suffering. I look down on the world and see how man stumbles along in sin. I look down on the world and cry.

I ask my children to listen. Prayer is the answer to all of your needs. Prayer is the answer to all of your questions. Prayer is the answer to all.

Sacraments are not to be forgotten or just taken as a duty. Sacraments should be seen as what they are, God's gifts. Sacraments are to strengthen, purify, cleanse, fill you. Sacraments are to bring you closer to God. Sacraments are essential to living.

Sacraments are special graces which help those in need, which help those in pain, which help those in trouble, which help all.

Sacraments should be taken often, daily if possible.

Sacraments are the most underrated gifts of God when they should be the most sought after.

Sacraments are for living. Sacraments are for all. Sacraments are from God.

Our Lady—12/11/94

Opening the door to Heaven is what the Lord Jesus did with His sacrifice. Defeating evil is what the Lord Jesus did with His giving; showing God's mercy is what the Lord Jesus does every time He brings His love to man.

ttt

Our Lady—12/11/94

Opposite the cross was a man, a man who loved God. This man was a special man, a true friend of Jesus. This man showed he loved Jesus no matter what the danger, no matter what the risk. This man, John, showed the true love that all have but most keep hidden. After the death of the Lord Jesus, John was my comfort, after the resurrection, John was by my side.

John, a man who trusted Jesus completely, loved Jesus completely, and gave himself completely to God through Jesus. John, when he wrote the Word of God, gave his personal testimony on the life, death, and resurrection of the only Son of God. John, who inspired so many to follow the true path, the path that is Jesus. John, who cared for others' souls as if they were his own. John, who bore much pain and suffering but bore it in the joy that is the love of God. John, my son, John my child, John, through whom mankind could see that I am mother to all.

✝✝✝

Our Lady—12/12/94

Sweetness is the taste of the love that Jesus brings. Sweetness is the taste of the joy that Jesus brings. And sweetness is the taste of Jesus for He is love and He is joy.

Our Lady—12/18/94

Loyalty, love, and truth are all needed when following the Lord Jesus. A loyalty that lasts forever, a love that endures for eternity, and a truth that traverses time.

✝✝✝

Our Lady—12/22/94

In the deepest recesses of your heart you will find a love that was put there by the Creator. In the corners of your mind you will find a truth that was put there by God. In the shadows of your spirit you will find a light that was put there by the Lord. The Lord God of Creation gave you a love, a truth, a light, that will never die, that will never leave, and that will never darken if you trust in His Son Jesus.

Our Lady—12/22/94

Looking in love at others is what Jesus did at all times. This is what you must try to do. If you see others with the eyes of love then you see them how you should. If you can remember that each man and woman is your brother, your sister, your family, then you see what mankind truly is, a family.

If you try to treat each person as if he is part of you and celebrate this oneness, then you can truly love life as it was supposed to be. In becoming a part of the family of man, the family of God, you became a part of a special people, the people who are God's children and who are destined to live forever with God. In accepting Jesus as your Lord, as the true Son of God, as God, you accept the truth that unites you with God forever.

Our Lady—12/23/94

Joy to the world for the Savior is near, hope for the Redeemer is near, hope for the world for Jesus is near.

Our Lady—12/29/94

Truth of Truths, Lord of Lords, God of Gods, Jesus. Light of Lights, Flame of Flames, Love of Loves, Jesus. Perfume of Perfumes, Flower of Flowers, Honey of Honeys, Jesus.

†††

Our Lady—12/29/94

Place your thoughts in my hands, place your love in my Heart, and place your spirit in my Spirit and I will give them to my Son Jesus as a gift.

Lay your heart on me, lay your life on me, lay yourself on me and I will comfort you, my dear son.

Caress my love with your soul, caress my soul with your love and become one with me in Jesus.

Falling down in adoration, falling down in love, falling down in delight, falling down in the arms of Jesus.

†††

Our Lady—12/30/94

Words of love were the first words Jesus spoke, words of love were the only words Jesus spoke, and words of love were the final words Jesus spoke on the cross.

A friend of Jesus are you. A son of God are you and a sweet fragrance of love you have become.

Trust in Jesus, trust in Love, and trust in your God.

Our Lady—12/31/94

Caressing my children .with love, holding my children with love, guiding my children with love, the love that is Jesus.

Our Lady—12/31/94

Jesus Christ, Son of God, Son of man, one in God and one in man, one in love and one in Mercy, one in joy and one in Glory, and one in Eternity.

Our Lady—12/31/94

A garment of love, a garment of faith, a garment of hope awaits those who believe in Jesus.

Our Lady—12/31/94

Rubies of love, drops of blood. Jewels of joy, tears of love. Diamonds of hope, words of God.

†††

Our Lady—1/1/95

Truth of truths is my Son Jesus. Love of loves is my Son Jesus. Light of lights is my Son Jesus and Friend of friends is my Son Jesus. He is the Truth, the only Truth. He is Love, the only Love. He is Light, the only Light and He is your friend, your true Friend who loves you and fills you with His Light.

Our Lady—1/1/95

The merciful Father sent His Son Jesus to the world as an act of love and forgiveness. The Holy Spirit sent His Son Jesus to Mary as a union between God and man. Loving Jesus came as a bridge between Heaven and earth. Now man needs to accept this Mercy, embrace this Holiness, and cross this bridge in a union of love that will last for eternity.

†††

Our Lady—1/4/95

Through the pain of sin shines a light, through the sorrow of suffering shines a love, and through the sadness of despair shines a saving grace; the Light of God, the Love of God, and the Grace of God.

Our Lady—1/4/95

Majesty, Truth, Love, Joy, Happiness, and Warmth of the Spirit, all describe my Son Jesus, for He is all good things; He is all graces and He is all God.

Our Lady—1/4/95

Leaning on my shoulder as a child was the Son of God. He leaned on me for support in His childhood; now it is man's turn to lean on me as little children and to receive my support and love.

Our Lady—1/6/95

Flower of Love, Flower of Joy, Flower of Heaven. Blossom in Love, blossom in Joy, blossom on the way to Heaven.

✝✝✝

Our Lady—1/6/95

Reaching within to find the Love of God that is living there.

Reaching within to find your true self in God's Love.

Reaching within to find true peace, the peace God, through His Son Jesus, has put there.

Our Lady—1/6/95

Snuggled in my arms close to my heart rested the Son of God. Clothed with love and joy, drenched with my affection, flooded with Joseph's admiration, and filled with God was the Lamb who came to take away man's sins. How this changed when He went through His passion.

Beaten by the arms of those He came to save, clothed in jest and abuse by those He loved, drenched in blood, shed for those He called His family, flooded with pain on the cross to deny the evil one his victory over man...filled with love throughout His passion, a love for His children whom He would save with His sacrifice to the Father in Heaven.

✝✝✝

Our Lady—1/16/95

Mother of Mercy, Maid of Love, Daughter of Desire. The Mercy and Love that is Jesus and the desire to serve God.

Our Lady—1/16/95

Nailed to the cross was my Son Jesus, pain filled His body and soul. As I watched an agony within burned so deep I could not stand. On my knees I prayed and prayed, on my knees I wept for my Son's agony to end, and on my knees I saw the glory of God. I saw how much God loves His children, how much He was prepared to give to save them and how much He needed to forgive them.

Nailed to the cross with my Son was my spirit, my being, my self. Nailed to the cross with my Son was my love, not as an equal but as a handmaiden wanting to serve her Lord and her God. In the service of Jesus was I, as I watched His supreme act of love, a service I long all to share with me so they can find the rewards that await them in Heaven, the rewards of God.

†††

Our Lady—1/17/95

Within your soul is a need, a need for love. Within your soul is a longing, a longing for love. Within your soul is a thirst, a thirst for love. Love is food for your soul and Jesus is Love.

Our Lady—1/18/95

A mother watches as her children struggle and as she watches she extends a helping hand, gently guiding to the right path. A loving touch from your Mother is waiting to help you; remember I am there for you.

Our Lady—1/18/95

My love is there for you, just hide yourself in it. My love is there for you, just wrap it around you. My love is there for you, just reach out in prayer and ask for it.

Our Lady—1/28/95

Close to me, close to you, close to all...that is God's love, a love to live by and a love to desire.

Our Lady—1/28/95

Long to live, long to love, and long to pray. Living is loving and loving is praying.

Our Lady—1/28/95

When my Son was in my arms as a child and I held Him close to me, I could feel His love filling my very being. As He held onto my hand and squeezed it in an expression of His love, my heart was filled with joy. When He opened His eyes and looked into mine, His love penetrated my very soul. When He snuggled into my embrace, His love opened my heart to God. This is how it should be every time you receive the Eucharist; you should accept and welcome the love of Jesus.

Our Lady—2/2/95

Flag of David, Flag of Truth, Flag of God.
Son of David, Son of Truth, Son of God.
Star of David, Star of Truth, Star of God.
Flower of David, Flower of Truth, Flower of God.
Jesus of David, Jesus the Truth, and Jesus is God.

Our Lady—2/2/95

Calling in love to the world, calling in hope to the world, just calling to the world because I love it. Asking for change, for change is needed, a change for the better. Asking for prayer, for prayer is needed, prayer for your souls. Asking for Sacraments, for Sacraments are needed for strength. Asking for love, for love is needed to exist. Asking for you to listen, for listening is needed to find the true destiny for mankind.

Chapter 2.

The Way With God—
Messages from God, The Father

God, The Father—10/3/94 & 10/4/94

There was a woman so pure, so sweet, so untouched by sin. This woman was sent by God to bear His Son, who would be the Redeemer of the world.

While still young and pure, the Lord came to this woman and asked if she was prepared to make the sacrifice of her whole life to save man by giving birth to the Son of God.

At first this young woman was frightened and then wondered if it was God speaking to her. After some time, she came to believe it was God, she knew it was God and so she offered herself freely and completely.

Her choice to do God's will was the choice that would bring God to earth as a man. Her choice was made out of her love and faith in God. Her choice was the most important choice ever made, for with this acceptance she brought forgiveness to mankind.

When she told her spouse Joseph, that she was with child, a child who was from God, who was God, Joseph doubted. It was only human that he should doubt, but after much prayer, an angel of the Lord came to Joseph and asked him to be a foster father, a guardian, a heavenly chosen protector to the Son of God.

Joseph who loved God dearly, immediately committed his life to doing God's work and accepted to be the earthly father to God. What Joseph did was to show his true love of God and his true faith in the Lord.

In a while Joseph and Mary were called to Bethlehem for the counting of names. It was a difficult journey, but they bore it with love and joy in God and in each other. They could not find a room to stay in and were offered a stable. Even with this difficulty, they thanked God for His mercy.

This stable became greater than any palace ever built. This stable became more than a stable; it became the beginning of salvation. The warmth in that stable on this bitterly cold night was warmer than all the fires in the world. The love in that stable was the greatest love the world has ever seen, and the light in that stable was the light for the world's redemption.

The time was here for the world to be saved. Here, in this humble setting was born the Son of God and the Son of man. Here, in this stable, was the living, loving, light of God. Here was God's gift to man— Himself.

With this one act God said to man that He truly loved man and because His love for man was so deep, He would be prepared to give His Son, Himself, as a sacrifice to save man.

The angels in heaven rejoiced, the Father rejoiced and the Holy Spirit rejoiced to see the Word made man, to see God's Son, born of a virgin born from an immaculate conception and born with true love for God and for man. This day was the one day when heaven came to earth, when God became man.

The child was named Jesus, the child was named Love...and the child was named Life. The child grew and grew, surrounded with love, the love of His mother who nurtured Him, the love of His foster father who protected Him and the love of God, His true Father who filled Him.

As He grew in years He grew in wisdom, God's wisdom. He grew in love, God's love and He grew in truth, for He is the truth. His years at home with his mother and Joseph were happy years. He filled His parents with joy, with ecstasy, with Him. They gave Him all of their love, all their joy, and all of their hearts. Every day was a blessing, every chore was a joy, every moment a gift of love, and every word a prayer. Complete living in God, with God, and for God. Completely at one with the Creator, the Spirit, and the Word.

This family, God's temple on earth, this God-Man on earth, this earth blessed by God.

The times were hard times, the times were difficult times, but the times were special times, for God was here on earth. The Romans occupied the sacred land. The Israelites were going further away from God. There were many false gods, false prophets, false teachings, and false people. Man lived mainly for himself. Man lived away from God and man even questioned God's word.

The times were evil times, murder, slavery, adultery, stealing, lying, fighting, drinking, lusting, and oh, so many sins were embraced by mankind.

God did not receive much praise, just much avoidance. God's laws were ignored as they were too hard to follow. It was easier to sin and it was so enjoyable. Who needed God when they could do what they wanted as long as they didn't offend Caesar?

Life was nothing. It was just to be lived and enjoyed and forget the consequences, forget your God, forget eternal life, forget everything except yourself.

†††

One day God's Son Jesus came forth and started to preach about God's love, God's laws, and God's life awaiting all in heaven. All of a sudden, people started to listen to this man, Jesus. They listened not because of what He was saying, but because of the miracles He performed. If they were sick, He could heal them, if they were possessed He could free them, and when He spoke, they felt good. Maybe, if they listened to Him it would be a short cut to heaven. Maybe they could carry on sinning, but still get to heaven.

When He spoke of repentance, they didn't really listen. When Jesus spoke of love, only a few listened. When He spoke of heaven, all listened for they all wanted to go there. After all, it was their right, for God had chosen them. They could do as they wanted as long as they made a few token offerings and God could accept them in heaven, for they were chosen.

The people came to Jesus for an easy way to God, an easy way to heaven and they found it. It was the way of love, for Jesus is love and it was the way of forgiveness, for Jesus is forgiveness and it was the way of God, for Jesus is God.

The more Jesus spoke and the more miracles He performed, the more people came to Him. This is what Jesus wanted—as many people to come to Him so that they could be saved.

Of those who came to Jesus, some stayed and some turned away. Those who stayed became the foundation of the new church of God, the Body of Christ. Those who stayed were given the feast of love, that is Jesus in the Eucharist. Those who stayed were the true sons and daughters of God. Those who stayed were welcomed in heaven by the Father.

Of those who stayed, twelve were chosen by the Lord Jesus to be His pillars on which to build His new church and to spread the good news. Eleven were true and one was false. One was filled with desire for glory on earth, with jealousy, with greed, and with deceit. Jesus knew this and still He loved him. The followers of Jesus were to be His light on earth, when He returned to the Father in heaven.

When Jesus spoke to these chosen ones, He told them all. He showed them all and He gave them all.

Once they understood who Jesus truly was, they would follow Him anywhere and give everything for Him. They loved Him, they worshipped Him, and they adored Him. All except one, one full of jealousy.

†††

The Lord led them to the truth of God, led them to the love of God, and showed them the way to heaven. Jesus gave them many gifts to use in His name. He showed them how to give their love to others freely. He showed them how to heal in His name and He showed them how to live in His name.

Jesus showed them all, so that when He was no longer with them, they could show others what He had shown them. Jesus graced these apostles so that they could bring His message to the world. Jesus came to the world for one reason—the salvation of man. Jesus came to the world for man and for God. Jesus came to the world to bring man back to God. Jesus came to the world for the redemption of mankind.

✝✝✝

To save man Jesus chose men. To save man Jesus chose men who were true of heart, who were sincere in their love of God. To save man Jesus chose men who would give their all for their God.

Jesus knew that when He had to leave them they would carry His word, God's word, to the world. Jesus knew they would at first falter when His time came, but then they would be strong for Him, in Him, and with Him.

Jesus knew His Spirit would flow through them freely and Jesus knew that they would take the Spirit to all mankind.

Jesus knew, for He knew all things. Jesus knew all they would or would not do and Jesus loved them. The day of the great betrayal came and the weak one succumbed to the devil. This so-called follower and friend of Jesus sold his soul for thirty pieces of silver. He rushed to do the evil one's bidding. He rushed to the servants of Satan, for this is what they were on this day. This day they turned against God.

It was only after Judas had betrayed the Lord that he came to understand what he had done. He had given the Son of God, the Messiah, the Redeemer into the hands of His enemies. He tried to undo what he had done, but to no avail. He could not live with what he had done. If only he had asked for forgiveness, it was there for him.

How Judas suffered within. How Judas suffered. He had betrayed God. He had betrayed Jesus. He had betrayed his brothers. What could he do now? How could he live? How could he exist? If only he had asked Jesus for forgiveness, all his sins would have been forgiven. If only he had asked Jesus.

Sweet Jesus gave His all for man. He gave Himself. He suffered abuse, scorn, beatings, humiliation, and finally death for man—what love!

Jesus, throughout His passion, thought of His love for man, His love for the Father in heaven and how He could break the chains of sin that bound man. Jesus was the sacrifice that would defeat sin forever. Jesus was the offering the Father needed to forgive man and Jesus was man and God, who was to lead mankind back to heaven. Mankind needed to be brought back, mankind needed to be shown how much God loved it, and mankind needed to be forgiven.

Mankind was given the greatest gift that God could give—Himself. Mankind was shown the greatest love, God's love, and mankind was given the greatest act of mercy, God's forgiveness.

When man begins to understand what God truly gave, when man understands why God truly gave, and when man understands what man must give in return, then man will know the way to God. The way to God is Jesus and only Jesus. There is no other way.

Jesus is the key to heaven. Jesus is the way to heaven. Jesus is the way to God. Jesus is God.

✝✝✝

It was time for man to follow the path of Jesus. Follow His path to the Father in heaven. It was time for man to follow the love of Jesus, follow His love to heaven; and it was time for man to follow the mercy of Jesus, follow His mercy to heaven. It was time for man to change, change into the being he was supposed to be—a being of love.

Jesus came back from the dead to show man that He was God...the true God with the Father in heaven and the Holy Spirit. Jesus came back and showed that heaven existed, that God existed and that He was the Messiah, the true Son of God.

What Jesus did when He was resurrected was to fulfill the Scriptures. What Jesus did when He came back to life was give mankind a glimpse of the next life that awaits man in heaven. What Jesus did when He came back to life was to show all mankind that if they listened to Him and followed His Word, they, too, could live life eternal.

When the Lord Jesus was lifted to heaven, He promised mankind that they, too, could be taken into heaven by proclaiming Jesus as Lord. When the Lord Jesus was lifted to heaven, He promised His Spirit to all mankind and He promised His love to all mankind.

The promises of the Lord Jesus are man's inheritance, man's birthright, man's treasure. All man has to do is claim them by proclaiming Jesus as Lord.

The Apostles gathered with the friends and followers of Jesus; Mary, His most Holy Mother was there too. They gathered to discuss what had happened and what to do. The Mother of God told them to trust in Jesus and all would be well.

The Holy Spirit of God filled all that were present with His fire. They were in ecstasy, full of joy, full of happiness, full of God. They went out and spoke to all in their own tongues. They touched their souls with God's Spirit and many came to understand that Jesus was Lord, Jesus was the true Son of God. Jesus was and is God, Jesus lives.

At that moment the gifts of God were given to the new church of God. The gifts of love, faith, hope, and charity. The gifts of the Spirit, the gifts of God. With these gifts, the Lord Jesus fulfilled His promises to His disciples. He told them He would send His Spirit who would fill them with God's graces and in His name they would be able to perform many wonders, many incredible acts, and many conversions.

These people, just ordinary people, showed what God's love could do. It could take any person, no matter who or what they were, where they came from, or what they did. It could change them into true followers of God's Son, Jesus.

Imagine what the people thought when they saw these followers of Jesus, full of love and joy, full of gladness, full of help, full of healing, full of sharing, just so full of love. No wonder so many wanted to become part of the good news. No wonder the old church shook. No wonder the empire shook, no wonder!

The joyful people of God made others think about Jesus. Was He truly the Son of God? If He was, we had agreed to His crucifixion. Many came and begged forgiveness and became His loyal servants. Many though, in their anger at themselves, turned to violence against the true believers. They persecuted them, they killed them, and they hated them. There were many who set about destroying these followers of Christ. There were many who hunted them down for rewards and there were many who just hunted them down out of spite.

Amongst these persecutors the Lord chose one to be His own, to be one of His lights in the world. Who better to choose than he who hates you? Who better to show your love to? What a man God chose! This man took the Word to the world and finally gave his life in Rome for God.

Paul, a man of faith, a man of God, and a man amongst men. With this act, Jesus showed how great was His love and His mercy. With this one act Jesus showed that anyone can be loved by God. All it takes is for them to accept God's love and God's love is Jesus. Jesus is Love and Jesus is Lord.

Knowing Jesus is Lord is the key that brought His followers into the Light and out of the dark. Knowing Jesus is Lord is what filled His followers with the power of God and knowing that Jesus is Lord is what saw His followers through their pain and suffering. Placing their lives in Jesus' hands is what brought them to heaven.

The Church has grown and grown since those early days, but the demands are the same. Love your God, love your neighbor and live a good life in God's commandments. The Church today must look back at the early Church and see the truths by which the first Christians lived. These truths are still valid today.

These truths are the truths man should live today, and these truths are still the way of God.

The followers of Jesus Christ today must look back at how the early Church lived in God's word and the Church today must live in the same word.

Today life is no different. It is only the surroundings that are changed. Today sin is no different. It is only the amount that has changed. Today the sacrifices required are no different. It is only man that has changed. Today man must think about how he has changed and with that change how he has lost many of the joys, the gifts, the graces of the Lord.

If men can look to the early Church and return to these values, then men can become true believers again.

†††

These are the words given to me
by The Holy Spirit,
who wants mankind to awaken to God.

Chapter 3.

The Way of God's Mercy—
Messages from God, The Holy Spirit

God, The Holy Spirit

In the beginning was God—God the Father, the Son, and the Spirit. In the beginning was the Holy Trinity. In the beginning was God. God filled the heavens with His angels, His love and His truth. God made all from His truth—Himself. God made all to be love; God made all to be truth.

In His love and wisdom the Father gave the angels freedom, freedom in His love. This freedom was a gift from God to His angels so that they could freely show their love. With this freedom some of the angels believed they were as God; some believed they were God's equal.

They did not understand what God had truly given them. They did not understand that God had allowed them to be full of His love when they accepted Him completely and freely. They did not understand that by denying God they allowed hate and anger into their spirits. Then, as they saw how the angels, who took God's gift and returned it to Him with thanks and praise, were rewarded by the Father, they became jealous.

Lucifer was the one who led these fallen angels in a revolt against God. Even with all the knowledge they had, they did not understand who God truly is. The Lord sent His true servants to defeat these unruly ones and in their defeat they have festered and grown in evil and hate. The evil ones still do not understand the true majesty, power, and love of God. It is beyond their comprehension; because of this they still believe they can defeat God. They believe they can defeat the truth, the love, and the Word of God.

God, who is complete love, became sad at the actions of these evil angels. He was unhappy that they could turn from His love, even though He knew it would happen. God's love was made complete again when He made man in His image, an image of love. God's love was fully appreciated by the first man, for Adam was one in God's love.

The Father, in His mercy, decided that man should have a companion to share and enjoy the gifts God had given. God created woman, woman and man, one in God's eyes. The love and joy in God and God's gifts brought happiness to the Father, brought joy to heaven, and brought life to earth...life in God. The animals were man's friends. They lived together playfully, joyfully, happily. Each day was a day of love, a day of God, and a day of joy. Man, one with God's love and one with the world.

The Father, who in His love and mercy had given the angels the choice to love God or not, gave man and woman the same choice. How could He not, for if He gave choice to the angels, then man, who is just below the angels, should have the same choice. The Father said to man, "If you love me you will not touch this tree. Everything else you may touch, but not this tree."

Man said to the Father, "We love You and we will not touch this tree because of our love for You."

The Father knew that man was weak and would succumb to the evil one, who would use all of his power to tempt God's children.

Man, in his weakness, was tempted and ate of God's tree. God was sad even though He knew this would happen. God was sad, for He loved man.

Man hid from God because he was ashamed. Man hid from God because he had broken his promise to God. If men had not touched this tree, then God would not have been in the position of sending His Son to redeem mankind, so this had to happen. The Lord was to come to earth to defeat evil and so the first sin had to be.

As time went on, man sank deeper and deeper into sin. Many forgot God, many forgot love, and many forgot their destiny in God. Among men arose those whom God chose to remind mankind that He existed and that He loved them. Among men arose the prophets of the Lord. These servants of God were sometimes listened to, but usually scorned, abused, and killed.

✝✝✝

Mankind was shunning God and embracing Lucifer, but throughout this, there were those who held true to God and were His followers. These were special children of God, sons of God, and sons of man.

These men carried God's love from generation to generation. These men brought God's word to the world. The truth of God was kept alive by these few who showed love for their God and who showed how to live in God's love.

While many did not follow God, the people were lost. Anger, hate, greed, immorality, and many other unhappy things occurred. They happened because most had lost sight of God. Many had lost sight of life, love, joy, truth, and happiness. To replace these gifts of God that had been lost, many searched elsewhere and where else from God is there, except the dark?

The evil one deceived many into worshipping false gods, gods of self, greed, lust, anger, hate. False idols, that all do one thing—lead man away from God. Idols that delight in man's pain and suffering, delight in man's immorality, and delight in taking man from God. How happy is the evil one when he can steal a soul from God, as he believes this brings him closer to victory—how foolish.

God watches His children and sees those who turn from Him and He is sad. God is God of mercy, God is God of forgiveness and it is there for mankind. Even though mankind has and will commit many sins, make many mistakes, all God wants is to forgive and love His children, to bring them to His glory in heaven.

Mankind is like little children who need to be shown, through love and kindness, the way to live. God shows this love and kindness through His Son, Jesus. All man has to do is imitate Christ and mankind will find the true meaning to life.

Mankind was put here by God to become His true love. Mankind was put here by God to become His children.

Mankind was put here by God to live for love, to live for God. In God mankind will find everything it desires, everything that is good for mankind. Man started to look away from God and has had to pay for this mistake. It is not God who makes man pay, but man himself and the evil one. God does not hurt man, God only loves man. It is when man turns to the dark that man suffers, for the evil one always demands payment. The evil one always takes more than he gives. Man has still to come to understand this. Man, in his naivety, lets the dark in. God is often blamed for the wrongs in the world, but this is not God's doing, it is man's.

Man has been given everything he needs to live in peace and joy, but man either destroys or changes these. Some men take more than is theirs and so others receive less. Those who have more are not satisfied and so they take more again and so those with less have even less.

There is enough for everyone, but man, in his foolishness, says there is not. While many waste in abundance, others starve in need. Man then blames God when man should look at himself and share, share his love, his heart, himself. If man did this all could live in plenty, all could live in joy, all could live free from sin, and all could live in God.

Mankind has been so foolish, often listening to the dark and not to God. Down through the ages sin has grown. It is so pervasive it encompasses the whole world now. Sin is so common now that it becomes accepted as the norm, it becomes accepted as goodness, as what is right. Sin is in the very air you breathe, the food you eat, the books you read—everywhere.

Sin is so complete now that it often goes unnoticed until it is too late. What a sad picture I paint but it is the truth. Out of this sadness can come joy, if only mankind wants it.

The joy that can be man's is the joy of God's forgiveness—mercy, love, and willingness to take man back into His arms. If man can come to understand what can be his, then sin will leave this earth, evil will disappear. It is all up to mankind with the free choice it has been given, with the love, and with the graces God has given to mankind.

The Father will never force His will upon man; He will only guide and advise, then He leaves it to man to decide his own future. God lets man determine his own destiny. God loves man and from this love comes God's will that man may choose freely, that man should see the right path and take it. There is only one path to God and that is through His Son, Jesus, and by following Jesus' example on how to live and how to give.

†††

Jesus is the way. Has man the love, the strength, the character, the will to walk this way? God knows man has, it is only man who denies it.

Down through time, the treatment God's messengers have received has always been harsh, it has always been a difficult task to serve God. The rewards in this life are few, but the glory in the next is great. Through time God has given His guidance to a few to share with the many. God has always asked the many to follow with faith alone. If all mankind would embrace true faith in God, then the path to heaven would be clear.

The prophets of the Lord know God, know His love, His wonder. They try to share this with all, only to be abused and mocked. Is it because the prophets speak truly and show man his sins and weaknesses

that mankind often resents them? Is it because God's
chosen ones are seen as special, as how all men want
to be, but cannot be, as it is too difficult to follow
their example? If others cannot be as they are, then
others make fun of, ridicule, abuse, and reject God's
chosen.

†††

Man turns from God, rejects, and abuses His
messengers and then crucifies God's Son. What
treatment of the Creator, what treatment of God! God,
in His mercy, still says to mankind that He loves
them, no matter how much man ignores or rejects
God. God, in His infinite mercy, is longing to forgive
His children and bring them home to Him in His
glory in Heaven. All man has to do is repent and
ask forgiveness and it is his; it is there if man wants
it, it is there if man seeks it. It is there.

What of man's destiny, what of man's future? It
is up to man, he chooses his destiny, his own future.
Mankind has two choices—light or darkness. Mankind
has two destinies—good or bad. Mankind has two ways—
right or wrong. There is no middle path, it is one
or the other. You cannot be with God sometimes,
usually when you need Him, then ignore God at other
times.

Man must come to understand you can only make
one choice. If you choose God, then you must stay
with God through good times and through bad times.
Man cannot spurn God when he feels he no longer
needs Him. If you choose God, then you must keep
all of His laws and not just the ones you agree with.
If you choose God, you must keep to His way, the
way of love, the way of Jesus, God's true Son.

If you turn from God to the dark, you must
understand what you turn to. You turn to pure hate,
evil, terror, torment, anguish. You turn to eternal
suffering, you turn to pain that never ends, you turn
to hell. It is not God that forces you there, but it
is yourself that accepts it freely, it is yourself who
asks for this, not God. So, when you turn from
God, look deeply to see what you really invite upon
yourself; look deeply and then repent and God will

save you through His ever loving Son, the Lord God Jesus Christ.

It is never too late if you truly seek forgiveness. It is never too late to ask for love and it is never too late to ask to change. So look wisely and make the right choice, the only choice, the choice of God, the choice of Jesus.

Why does the world suffer so, for there are many who love God, there are many who live good lives, and there are many who help and love others? Yes, there are many good people, but there are also many lost, misled, confused, or just evil people. The majority of people are good, but sit quietly by as sin grows in the world.

The truly evil ones confuse the majority and lead them into sin, sin that is often so sublime it no longer seems like sin. The evil ones put a smile on the face of evil and then it looks like reason.

Abortion, wars, starvation, greed, new age, drugs, immorality, all can now be justified, but all are against God, all are sins, but somehow they seem not to be. They have become the acceptable face of evil, but they are still evil, regardless.

When mankind can understand what this evil does, then man will see why the world suffers so. How many good people accept these sins and make excuses for not standing against them? This turns good people from God and into the Evil One's hands because they accept his will. They accept these sins and say, "They are not sins any more, they are now all right. They do not offend God. It was only man who made these as sins and so man can now accept them as part of life, as part of living. If there is a good reason all are acceptable, all are permissible, all are allowed in God's love, and all will be within God's wishes."

How can sinning be acceptable to God? How can man believe it would be? How can man think for God?

This is man placing himself as an equal to God just as the fallen angels thought they were God's equal. Will man have to learn as the angels did? Will man have to be shown the truth of God? Will man have to be brought to his senses so that he can be saved from hell? God wants to save man, God wants to show man His mercy, God wants to bring man to His salvation, His salvation, that is, Jesus. If man will take the time to listen to the Word of God, Jesus, then man will know what he has to do to overcome the weight of sin on the world.

†††

When sin is lifted from mankind then the path to God will be so clear to all that they will wonder why they didn't reject sin before. What is sin? Sin is the chain that keeps man from God. It is a self-made chain that is encouraged by the dark.

If mankind could turn to Jesus and find its strength in His suffering, His passion, His crucifixion, then man could defeat evil.

Mankind should be able to see that the Lord Jesus has already defeated evil with His giving of Himself. It is just up to man to accept this, to believe this, and to praise this. When man does this, evil will not be able to seduce, deceive, or confuse man. Evil will be put to rest in hell where it belongs. Evil will no longer exist, evil will no longer be.

What a future can be mankind's if only it rejects sin and evil, accepts God, accepts Jesus, accepts the Holy Spirit.

What joy can be mankind's if only it turns its back on the dark and turns to the light.

What glory can be mankind's—a shared glory, a glory in God.

What happiness can be mankind's, happiness for eternity with and in God.

What a future; just reach out for the Creator's love, the love that is forgiveness that is Jesus Christ and reach out for God's mercy, the mercy that is Jesus Christ.

Jesus is the answer to all. Jesus is the love for all and Jesus is God for all.

†††

These are the words given to me
by God the Son,
who loves man dearly
and is the way to eternal joy.

Chapter 4.

The Way to Eternal Love—
Messages from God, The Son

Lord Jesus

In a time not so long ago the whole world lived
in spiritual darkness, lost to God, lost to life in God.
Then the Father, in His mercy, sent His Son to light
up the world with God's love, God's word, God.

The Son came to show man how to live, to live
in God's way, to live in God's love, to live in God.
The Son came and opened the door to heaven for
those who would listen, opened the door to eternity
in love for those who believed, opened the door to
God for those who would follow.

These people who listened, believed, and followed the
Son, were to be shown the truth of God, the truth
that is Jesus. They were shown how Jesus fulfilled
the Word of God in the Old Testament and how He
was the living Word of God. Jesus showed them the
truth of the Word, how the Word was to be followed
and lived. Jesus gave a new word, a word of love,
love of God and love for each other. Jesus showed
how life was meant to be lived, how life was supposed
to be.

With the deep love Jesus had for mankind, He wanted to explain the mystery, the truth, the Love of God. Jesus wanted to lead man to a complete living in God, to a complete living for each other, and a complete living with joy.

What gifts Jesus brought for man, what graces He presented to man, what glory He gave to the Father!

Inside man is a love, a love which is often kept hidden. It is smothered with man's need to be self sufficient, in charge of his own destiny, his own master.

What mankind does not understand is that this love he smothers will give him true independence, true freedom, true happiness. Man knows he has this love inside, he knows it is there, but he does not know what it truly means.

This hidden love is the love God planted within mankind, it is the special grace that brings man to God, it is a blessing from God.

With this love man can free himself from sin, sorrow, pain, and suffering. Mankind can live in happiness and be truly free, mankind can live in joy and be truly independent, mankind can live in love and remain in charge of his own destiny, his destiny in God.

When this love is kept hidden, mankind is not free, mankind binds himself with the chains of sin and evil, mankind locks himself into an eternity of suffering. When this love is rejected, people become slaves of the dark, slaves of the world, and have little control over their destiny.

What is this love, this grace, this gift that is so powerful, so encompassing, so strong? It is God's Love, Jesus, it is God's Son, Jesus, it is God, Jesus.

To open the world to freedom, to open the world to joy, to open the world to its true destiny, open the doors of your hearts, your souls, yourselves to Jesus and be free.

Why has this love been hidden? Why has it been smothered? Why has it been ignored? It seems strange that mankind should turn its back on the beauty and joy of God's Love. What has blinded man and taken him from God?

Take a look around the world and see. It is obvious, it is everywhere, it abounds, it is man's self. Mankind now thinks only of himself, how can I better myself, how can I have more, how can I be successful, how can I get what others have?

It doesn't seem to matter any more what price man has to pay as long as he improves his own situation. If giving life to many children restricts one's lifestyle, one's enjoyment, one's aspirations, one's finances, one's future, then man says let's not have them and if God gives them the gift of life, man rejects it and kills it because it may inconvenience them.

If sharing your wealth with others stops you enjoying life, dining out, holidays, fast cars, big houses, fancy clothes, money to waste, then some men say, don't share with others. It doesn't matter that others starve, die from simple diseases which could have been treated, live in cardboard boxes, eat from rubbish, drink filthy water. Many men do not worry about these as long as they are all right.

If the poor seem to threaten your easy life, then mankind spends more on weapons to control them than it would cost to feed them, spends more on security than it would cost to house them, and spends more on entertainment than it would cost to cure them.

The love hides beneath the layers of self that man has created. Each moment these layers grow and grow as most men sit back and accept them. By accepting them, more layers are created. By accepting them, more sin accumulates. What in earlier times would have been rejected by mankind is now accepted by most. What in earlier times would have been considered evil, now seems good. All in the name of self. All in the name of the rights of man which really are the wrongs of man.

Man's individual privacy, man's individual rights, man's individual actions are all acceptable names for evil when immoral acts are condoned within these parameters. The saying, "Do what you like as long as it does not hurt anyone," is a saying from the dark. What happens is that the acts that do offend, eventually become acceptable, become the norm. How can anyone judge which acts will hurt another or not? How can anyone say it is all right, it was done in love between consenting adults so it will not offend anyone? How can anyone put themselves up as the authority on what is right or what is wrong unless they have that authority from God?

Man should remember that his authority, his laws, his justice carry no weight unless they are those proclaimed by God. The laws of God are plain to see. Many prophets have spoken them, many people have read them, but many people only accept what is suitable to them. When Jesus proclaimed the word He did not say, "These are God's commandments but only follow those that you agree with." He said, "You must follow them all."

†††

Mankind now needs to make a decision, a decision of love, love of God and love of fellow man. Mankind now needs to take himself by the hand and walk in love together, together with God. Mankind now needs to turn all his hopes and aspirations from self to others, hoping and aspiring that the whole of mankind can live in the love and peace of God.

What a wonderful future it can be for man if he is prepared to step forward in love, in joy, and in sharing. What a wonderful future it can be for man as he ascends the stairway to eternity together in love. What a wonderful future it can be for man if he will embrace his Creator's love and kindness, what a future for man.

Mankind was put on earth for this reason and this alone—to come to God in heaven, in love, for eternity. Accepting this brings man to the understanding of how he must live, how he must be. When mankind can see himself as he really is and how he should be, when mankind believes truly in God, his Creator, when mankind acknowledges he is here by God's grace, and when mankind respects God's wishes, then, and only then, can mankind find his true destiny, the destiny that God has prepared for man. Jesus explained how to do this. Jesus was an example of how to live in God's way. Jesus was what all men should aspire to be like.

Jesus gave His all to show mankind the way, Jesus gave everything to change mankind, and Jesus gave His entire being as an atonement for man's sins. Do not reject this sacrifice; accept it and accept God's love, for Jesus is God's love.

Wherever mankind looks he will find two paths, the path of self and sin or the path of God and love. Wherever man expects to be in the future, he will reach it by walking one of these paths. Wherever mankind wants his purpose for existing to be, it is along one of these paths.

The choices are obvious, the choices are so different it should be easy to choose; the choices are so wide apart that no wrong steps should be taken.

Mankind blurs the choices with his weakness; mankind blurs the choices with reason, reason that is really denial; mankind blurs the choice with other choices which are only one choice, evil.

What is man to do to make the right choice, to take the right path, the choice and path that leads to God?

What is man to do to avoid the grasping claws of the evil one, who waits to shred man's soul? What is man to do to pass from this life to the next in God's love? What is man to do?

The answer is there for all to see, the answer is clear to those who wish to see, the answer is there for all those who wish to hear, the answer is there for all those who wish to hear from their heart, from their soul, from within. The answer is Jesus, the answer is love, the answer is joy. The answer is God. It is an answer many deny, but it is the only answer, the answer of God's Son who came to help man choose the right path. Has man the ears to hear, the eyes to see, and the heart to follow?

Men of the world, women of the world now listen to the words of the one who loves you so deeply, so strongly, so passionately that He gave His life for you:

"My Dear Little Children,

"Look to Me now for help, look to Me now for forgiveness, look to Me now for love, for I am love.

"I ask you to reassess your lives, to look and see what you may be doing wrong, what you may be accepting that is wrong or what you are ignoring that is wrong. Stand up and speak for good, speak against evil, stand up for God. If My children will not stand up for Me, whom shall I ask? If My children ignore Me, who will listen? If My children sin, how can others be asked not to?

"My children, I shed My blood for you, I gave My life for you and I gave eternity to you, now accept it and take it. Take it by living to My word, living for God and for others, living for life eternal.

"Now is the time to stand under My banner, lift your voices against evil and show you are true sons and daughters of God."

†††

Part II

The Obvious Way

Chapters: Page:

1. The Sins of Mankind—   53.
   Messages from God, The Father

2. Under the Name of Reason—   67.
   Messages from Our Lady

3. Misunderstanding The Way—   70.
   Messages from God, The Father

4. The Way Home—   80.
   Messages from God, The Holy Trinity

Chapter 1.

The Sins of Mankind—
Messages from God, The Father

God, The Father—1/3/95

If there was ever a time mankind needed to look at itself and its morals, it is now.

Mankind now treads the path of despair due to a lack of morals, due to a lack of understanding of the value of life.

In the beginning, God gave mankind a set of morals that were built into his make up; a set of guidelines on how to live in the love of God and with each other. Over time mankind slipped little by little away from these morals. Then the Lord, through His loyal servant, Moses, reminded man what was required to live the good life.

Once again, mankind listened for a while and then little by little slipped away again. Then in the greatest act of mercy and love, God sent His Son Jesus to remind man where his true destiny lay. Jesus came and lived the life that all men should try to live. Jesus came and clearly showed the way to the Father in Heaven. Jesus came and forgave man and held out His hand to mankind in an act of love, a love that was from the Father, through Jesus and finally brought alive by the Spirit of God.

Jesus came and pointed mankind in the direction that was to lead to God. When Jesus pointed the way He showed that all mankind needed to do to achieve eternal happiness was to live in love, an unconditional love that would help, forgive, understand, and welcome others as you would expect to be welcomed yourself.

Now once again, mankind has slipped little by little from his God. Now mankind has created a society that lacks true morals but has many false morals; morals that are really sins, morals that are a denial of God, and morals that are an insult to Jesus.

When Jesus walked this earth, He only spoke of love, He only spoke of kindness, and He only spoke of truth. He told those who would listen of the sanctity of life; He told those who would listen of the warmth of love that was to be found in children. He told those who would listen to be as little children and they would achieve eternity in heaven.

Imagine how your Lord and God feels now as He looks down upon mankind and sees the children killed in wars, killed with starvation, and killed by abortion. All of which are avoidable but man chooses to propagate them, man chooses to keep them on the earth as a running sore that festers and festers.

Imagine how sad Jesus must be to see His little children abused so. Imagine how Jesus would want to reach out and stop all this hatred and all this sin.

Jesus has given man a choice; imagine how disappointed He is every time the wrong choice is taken.

God, the Father—1/3/95

ABORTION

Jesus has been watching mankind from creation and will continue to watch over mankind until the end of time. He knows each soul, each spirit individually. He knows each person individually and He calls each one His friend. No matter what each one does, he or she is still Jesus' friend but it is up to the individual to accept this friendship and become the love he or she was created to be.

As Jesus knows each spirit individually then imagine the pain He suffers when His friend's time on this earth is stopped before it is started. At the moment of conception the spirit enters the body, even if it is so minute that you cannot see it, the body is there and it is filled with the spirit God has created to be this person.

This spirit has all the feelings, understanding, and hope that a fully developed person has but mankind does not recognize this. When the spirit enters into its body, it already is complete in God because it comes from God; it already is a perfect creation which is about to go through the experience of living in a human body so that it can show freely that it loves God. Each spirit is from God's glory and is created to return in glory to God by following Jesus and by living to God's ways. What a gift from God creating, giving, loving, and finally bringing home to heaven His spirits of love, mankind.

Over time man has returned to the ways of immorality and now calls it a person's rights. The rights of the unborn spirits are ignored with the justification that the parents were not ready for children or they could not afford to have children.

Sometimes medical justifications are given such as: she is too young to have a baby, her body is not ready for it, she could not cope emotionally or mentally. These excuses and many more are used to cover up the sin that brings so much pain and suffering to all, the sin of Abortion.

Man turns what should be a celebration of the gift of life from God into a tragedy with the stain of sin that touches all involved. Abortion now becomes another form of contraception, it is promoted freely to all, it is considered as a safe alternative which should be available to all. Centers are established to promote the benefits of abortion instead of promoting the benefits of bringing life into the world. Satan's servants speak freely on this abomination, speak as if it is a wonderful gift to mankind that can help with the social and economic problems of many.

Those who promote this mortal sin use many clever arguments, many scientific and social arguments to show why this sin should be accepted and welcomed.

Each person knows deep within, this is a sin, this is against God's wishes but many listen to the clever arguments of the dark and let this inner knowledge become clouded and hidden. The message that this sin of murder is acceptable is fed over and over again to the world in the newspapers, on television, in movies, through world bodies and leaders of nations.

No wonder many are confused, no wonder many are lost. Where are the voices of love that stand for God? They are there but they are branded as fanatics or as extremists when in fact the reverse is true. What Satan has done to harm the voices of God, is to place within these groups, his servants, who by their cunning, confuse God's servants, confuse their words and actions so that it is easy to make them appear in the wrong.

If those who speak out and stand up for God remember God is love and all actions in His name must be actions of love, then the world will start to listen. It is when those who do God's work use the instruments of the dark to achieve their wishes, i.e., the shooting of workers in abortion clinics, that they no longer do God's work but the evil one's. God's servants must be seen as lights in the dark and to do this they must live as God has shown through His Son Jesus—no sin just love, no hate just mercy, no self-interest just helping others, and no desire except the desire to do God's work.

†††

Over time, the killing of innocents, born or unborn, seems to have little importance. The more abortions that are performed, the more justified they appear, the more abortions that take place, the more clever arguments are made to excuse them. The more often this sin takes place, the less it seems like a sin.

Consider what cost abortion has, what payment it demands, this sin of sins. First the sweet innocent is caused to suffer by the pain caused to its being. The pain when the body is destroyed, sometimes torn to pieces and then disposed of as rubbish. Sometimes well formed bodies are wrenched from the warmth and security of their mothers' wombs only to be made into lifeless flesh not wanted, not loved, not permitted to live. How these little ones cry out to be loved, how these little ones cry out to be wanted, and how they cry out to the Lord for His help. Now consider the effect on the spirit of the mother, she may not recognize or understand what she does to herself. Sometimes the payment is demanded later in her life with emotional and psychological problems; sometimes physical problems, but always spiritual problems... spiritual problems that will destroy her being if she does not ask the Lord Jesus for His forgiveness. Even if the mother does not believe it is wrong, it doesn't change the fact that it is, and that it is an insult to God.

Those who perform these dreadful procedures will be held to account for what they do. They will find all those whom they have destroyed waiting for the Lord's justice to be given when these corrupt ones face their Maker. Then it will be too late to ask for God's mercy. Now while they live on earth is the time for God's forgiveness. Now is the time to stop this terrible act and turn to their God and ask for His mercy. They know what God asks of them; if they ignore this, they do so at their own risk.

Those who condone these sins carry the blame as much as those who perform them. To agree with sin is to become part of it, to encourage sin is to promote evil, and to promote evil is to turn from God.

Why is it that it is always the weakest and most vulnerable who are the ones to suffer and usually suffer at the hands of the so called "do-gooders?" "Do-gooders" who can promote sin in any form for any reason are not "do-gooders" but are "do-what-you-wanters" as long as it harms no one i.e., promote abortion as acceptable. Unfortunately, it always harms someone and always the weak and vulnerable.

So these "do-gooders" are really servants of sin, servants of evil, servants of Satan even if they do not recognize it or admit to it. When these people see what they truly are doing and the harm they cause and ask for God's forgiveness, and start to undo the harm they have done, then God will shine His mercy into their souls, into their hearts, and into their spirits. It is up to them to choose God's forgiveness and God's love, and it will be there for them through God's Son Jesus.

Under the direction of their hearts, mankind will find the true answers to all the sins they commit. If mankind can let their true feeling shine through the hard outer layers that cover mankind's hearts and souls, then they can come to understand what is wrong and what is right. As these layers are peeled away the true man will be seen, it is up to man to peel these layers away with the love of Jesus. If there is not a re-assessment of what mankind is doing to themselves with the slaughter of the innocents, then the account will have to be paid and the cry of the innocents answered.

†††

The innocents are not only those who are killed by the most atrocious sins of abortion, but it is also those who starve because of man's indifference. It is also those killed innocently by man's aggression through wars, genocide, and repressive regimes. Every time a young one dies because of mankind's sins another debt accumulates and needs to be paid. Each time a young one is denied the opportunity to reach a full life in God, a soul cries out in despair and asks God why does its own family, the family of man, deny it.

Each time the children are tortured and killed, the angels in heaven cry out in love for this to be stopped. Each time a new life on earth is thought of as worthless, God's mother sheds tears of blood and wraps her arm around these spirits to comfort them and bring them to God in heaven. Each time man sins he brings himself closer to hell but does not believe it. Each sin is a step closer to the evil one's grasping claws but mankind closes its eyes to this.

Mankind with the encouragement of Satan commits these terrible acts, these offenses to God and to the spirits in heaven. Mankind embraces and welcomes sin, welcomes the evil one but will mankind welcome the payment when it is demanded? Does mankind think it will not be required to face its sins and to answer for them? How cunning is evil to deceive man so and

how foolish is man for not opening his eyes to what
is really happening. What is really happening is the
destruction of mankind by his own hands, by his
willing participation in the evil one's plans. How
foolish is mankind to think there is no evil one, there
is no Satan, what a clever trick the evil one plays
but what a stupid man to let him trick mankind over
and over.

Mankind must now shake free of the bondage of
sin that he has allowed to exist. He can start by
loving the children, not despising them. He can start
by saving the children, not killing them and by
encouraging life, not stopping it. He can start by lifting
his self-imposed cross from his back by turning to
God in prayer and asking for the Lord's forgiveness
and guidance. He can start by turning to Jesus and
taking His hand and walking along the path of love
with Him.

God, The Father—4/2/95

TRUTH

Truth today is very hard to find for even the
simplest truth is often changed, then it is no longer
truth.

Truth seems lost in today's world, even those who
lead nations lie openly and profess it is the truth
until it is discovered not to be. How can mankind
lead truthful lives if its leaders, its government, and
yes, often, its religious leaders do not tell the truth?

One of the commandments I gave through My
servant, Moses, and was later re-stated through My
own Son, Jesus, is, "Thou shalt not lie." I did not
say, "Thou shalt not lie when it suits you, but you
may lie at other times." I said, "Thou shalt not lie."
There is no justification for lying even if it is thought
to be in the best interest of those concerned.

How can a sin ever be in the best interest? A
sin can only be in the worst interest. To lie to cover
up other sins or mistakes only magnifies the problem,
only propagates sin. If the truth is told it stops sin
in its tracks, it stops sin festering and spreading.

The truth is the way of overcoming evil for it cannot face the truth, it runs and hides from it. Truth is what mankind must now try to return to as it is this that will stop the world sliding into the abyss of the dark.

Truth is a grace I have given you, I gave it to you to use not to deny. Now use truth as it was meant to be used, use it in love.

God, The Father—4/2/95

ADULTERY

To take another's spouse, another's partner in love, is to break another commandment I have given. "Thou shalt not commit adultery," is a commandment I gave, because man and woman become one in My eyes when they take the vow of marriage. This vow is taken before Me. It is a promise to Me that joins man and woman in love. This vow is a sacred oath which cannot be broken, this vow is a placing of both their souls as one into My heart.

This vow is a gift to Me from man and woman. A gift which magnifies in love every day they share. It is a gift which increases day by day the joy it brings Me. It is a gift which I treasure and hold close to My heart. It is a gift which I never want to lose, which I want to be with Me always so that I can look upon it and enjoy its purity and love. This gift is one of the most special gifts mankind can give to Me.

The destruction of marriages is an affront to Me for it takes away the gift I have given. The evil one knows this and so tries to destroy all marriages as an insult to Me. When adultery is committed, it is not only the marriage that is damaged but also those outside the marriage who take part in this sin. They are saying to their God, "I do not care about You; I do not care about my brothers and sisters; I only care about myself." It is not only those who actively participate in the adultery that are sinning, but also those who watch quietly and say nothing or even encourage it.

When a marriage is destroyed by adultery, the sin is so deep, so offensive to Me, your God, that I turn away in sorrow for I cannot bear to look upon it.

At times these lost children of mine re-marry and then believe that they no longer sin, for in the eyes of mankind they are man and wife. How the evil one has deceived My children for they live in a constant state of sin which is worse day by day. They do not recognize this sin, their friends and families often do not recognize it and just accept it. Again, sin grows and spreads, affecting all those it comes in contact with. Those who live in this state of sin must seek forgiveness through My Son Jesus, and when they receive this forgiveness they should not return to sin.

†††

Sometimes marriages fall apart for other reasons, reasons of violence, anger, selfishness, greed, unkindness, so many reasons but all are reasons which come from the evil one.

In a marriage, if the love is nurtured and fed, kept in the front of your minds and hearts, then none of these would happen for love defeats all. Unfortunately, in their weakness, My children often succumb to the evil and do not let their love shine through. If this happens and one half of this marriage decides to leave, the other must remain true to the promise made before Me. If they do not, then they are drawn into sin as well. They must continue to live as if their spouses are still with them; in this way, they show their true love of their God and of their chosen ones. Their gift is then very special to Me and in return, I keep a special place in My heart for them.

Mankind must remember that to unify in love before God is a very special grace. This grace must never be rejected or destroyed, for if it is, then you damage your soul, your spirit grievously.

†††

God, The Father—4/2/95

LIFE OR DEATH

"Thou shalt not kill," is another commandment I have given to My children. Why would I give this commandment? Why would I say to kill is wrong? The explanation is very simple, if you kill another knowingly, then you destroy My creation, a creation of love. Not only do you destroy My creation in another but you destroy your very soul, you deny yourself eternal life in heaven.

There are many ways of killing and many excuses for it but whatever the way, whatever the reason, it is still wrong, it is still a sin. If you kill for justice or for what is right, this is a sin. If you kill for truth and honor, this is a sin; if you kill for revenge or for your country, this is a sin. All killing is a sin unless it is an accident, unless it was not meant to happen.

The taking of a life no matter what the reason offends Me your God deeply and it scars your soul mortally.

Those who agree to killing, whether it be through their governments in wars or in justice, carry the scars on their souls also. Those who agree to killing as an act of mercy, as an act of help for those in pain, still carry this scar on their souls. Those who stand by and watch as others kill and say nothing, by their inaction scar their very souls. Those who kill to stop killing become the same as those they oppose, they become filled with sin. All killing is wrong, all killing offends Me your God and all killing leads you away from God.

God, The Father—4/2/95

GREED & ENVY

Man sins so much because of his greed and envy of others. Mankind always wants more, more, more. No matter what he has, he always strives for more. This can be a grace if it is more love, kindness, joy, truth, happiness, and faith that is sought. It becomes a sin when it is more for self and less for others, when it is more to waste instead of more to share, when it is more for personal glory and less of God's glory, when it is more than is needed.

Mankind looks at others and sees what they have and says, "I want that," then takes it regardless of how their brothers and sisters are hurt, regardless of how the animals or the planet are hurt, regardless of all.

So many sins are committed because of greed and envy, so much pain and suffering, so much that takes man from God and takes man to eternal darkness.

Greed and envy must change to become giving and enjoying what you have, then mankind can once again walk the path that leads to heaven.

God, The Father—4/2/95

IMMORAL ACTS

When God created mankind, God created man for woman, and woman for man. Mankind has been created this way so that man and woman in love can become one with God. Mankind has been created that way to bring love into the world in My little ones. Mankind has been created for man to fertilize with his seed and woman to carry within her body, the future of mankind. Man is one half of the equation, woman, the other. Both equal and both joined to be one with God in creation. If it was to be any other way, then God would have made it so.

Those who live life immorally with partners of the same sex are offensive before God and are offensive to all of creation. Their immoral acts take their very spirits into the hands of the evil one. This offence to God, to all, has now become acceptable to many, even to the extent that it is paraded in the streets. It is acceptable by man's law and it is even recognized as family. The more it is given approval, the more people will be attracted to it. Isn't this the way of evil?

Many weak or vulnerable people are led by the dark to this way of life, which really is a way of eternal death. Many weak and vulnerable people are deceived into believing that it is all right to behave this way.

What these people need is love and understanding to guide them back into the light of God. It is every Christian's duty to do what he can to help these lost children find their God again.

How the evil one smiles each time a soul turns to this depravity, this evil which hurts God deeply! How the evil one smiles as many are so easily led down this path! How the evil one smiles as mankind closes his eyes to this sin, how he smiles!

God, The Father—4/2/95

SUBSTANCE ABUSE

The bodies mankind were given are temples of God. Each body was given to mankind to treasure and to keep pure for God. Each body was designed to meet all the needs that man has physically; each body was designed by God.

When substances that are not for the well being or the health of the body are taken, this is saying to God, "I don't respect Your gift to me."

Anything that is taken and is not for the fulfillment of God's love within the temple, that is the body, is from the evil one and is sent to destroy. These substances appear so attractive; they make you feel good, they make you forget your problems, they make you ecstatic but payment is often more than you know. The payment can be your soul, your very spirit.

Isn't this the way of sin, so attractive at first but always demanding payment?

If only mankind would look to God and open themselves completely to His love, then they would find all the excitement, love, good feelings, ecstasy that they could possibly want. Being filled with God's love is beyond comparison and once seen is never to be lost.

God, The Father—4/2/95

MANKIND'S CHOICE

It seems then that mankind is lost in sin, for most either sin, live in sin, accept sin or ignore sin. Most no longer see sin as sin but just see it as part of life or part of man's search for his destiny. Sin becomes a partner to many in life and becomes a chain to many in death.

Sin has grasped the world in its hands and the world in its weakness and blindness welcomes it. Mankind closes its hearts to love and goodness and opens its hearts to sin and suffering.

Over centuries sin grows and grows, it never really changes. It is the same sin now as in the days of Sodom and Gomorrah; it is the same sin now as in the days of Moses; it is the same sin just under different names with different reasons for accepting it.

Sin is in the very air you breathe, the food you eat, the drugs you abuse yourselves with, the so-called love you have in immoral relationships; the contraception and abortion you use to gain a better life on earth, the wars mankind has either in so called justice or in hate; the killing of the young and the old, the killing of the disabled or infirmed, the killing of those who want what you have; the changing of creation to suit mankind's needs, the altering of God's design for the world, the denial of God and the rejection of God's commandments.

The world swims in sin, the world opens its arms and embraces the evil one and his servants. The world has been warned over and over again, it has been shown the results of sin with all the wars, famines, plagues, and disasters that occur and yet, still it embraces and welcomes sin. Many in the world become Satan's slaves knowingly or unknowingly.

The Lord your God now asks mankind to re-assess how it lives, how it exists. Re-assess what it accepts and what it denies, what it adopts as its laws and what it enforces upon itself. Mankind needs to think long and hard about what it invites upon itself and what it will do when payment is demanded.

Your God asks you to look to His Son Jesus, look to your Savior, your Redeemer and ask for His mercy.

Those who live in sin, live immorally, commit immoral acts, break God's commandments, spurn God, deny God, and destroy themselves, must take a moment and look at their lives; take a moment and look at their sins and take a moment and look at their future; then decide if they wish to live life eternal in joy and love or in pain and suffering.

Those who make the right choice and turn to Jesus for His forgiveness will find it waiting for them. Jesus longs to help all of God's children, His children. Jesus longs to help, just ask Him, just ask Him.

ttt

Chapter 2.

Under The Name of Reason—
Messages from Our Lady

Our Lady—3/19/95

(Smell of roses. Then Our Lady asked me to write.)

So many sins today are accepted under the name of reason. So many wrongs are seen as right. This is how evil works, it makes bad seem good and good seem bad. Evil turns love into an abomination, evil turns righteousness into something to be scorned and turns lies into truth. How cunning is evil, so clever, so tantalizing, so appealing; always attacking mankind at its weak points—weaknesses of pride, selfishness, greed, laziness, vanity—and in so many more ways the evil one can deceive and lead mankind away from God's love.

If mankind would only open its eyes and see the evil that abounds throughout the world, see how easily evil is spreading. Today, even from a very young age, mankind is taught to accept evil and to see it as exciting, as glamorous, as fulfilling all of its needs. Mankind shows the young through entertainment that evil is an acceptable choice, this turns entertainment from what it should be into an instrument of the dark. When children see adults involved in crime, violence, or sexual abuse in so-called entertainment, then they start to see it as acceptable behavior, for if the adults condone it, enjoy watching it, find it exciting, then it must be all right to behave that way. Children follow the example of their elders and if they see bad things accepted as good by their parents or older friends, then they accept them as good. How clever is the evil one in educating the young in his ways and educating them in evil through the ones who love them.

As the young grow with these values that they have so subtly been taught, they then live them—murder, stealing, drugs, rape, adultery, lies, hate, anger, and violence become the way of life for some. Most accept some of these and others accept all. Look at the crimes committed in the name of national security or ethnic rights, nothing is forbidden. However, there are those who stand for peace, stand for God, stand for love, stand for hope, stand for goodness but look what happens to them. These people who seek the true way for man to be are often beaten, killed, humiliated, scorned, proclaimed as weak and useless. Isn't this how evil has always reacted to goodness? It cannot stand against it so it takes as many away from it by using its cunning to make good look bad, evil seem right.

It is so obvious how evil reacts. It has been the same since time began but mankind closes its eyes to it. Evil has been so blatant and yet mankind still does not see what evil is and how it tricks mankind into destroying himself.

Mankind must now stop and look at what is allowed to happen to its children and itself. What a future awaits mankind if it follows the path of sin and evil; these can only lead to one destiny, an eternity of suffering, an eternity in the dark, an eternity away from God's love.

If mankind can open his heart and see the beauty, the joy, the happiness, the love that can be his by joining with his Creator through His Son Jesus' heart, then mankind can reach for its true identity, true self, true spirit; the identity that is love, the self that is for others' needs, the spirit that is freedom—freedom in God's love, freedom that enables mankind to become clothed in the garments of God's mercy and grace.

Walking hand in hand with Jesus, mankind will see how the evil one deceives, mankind will see the vast difference between good and evil, mankind will remove the mask from his eyes, the stone from his heart and the evil in the world will become so obvious that it will sicken mankind to see what he has accepted, to see what he has been denying. The cross mankind now carries will be lifted, and on that glorious day sweet Jesus' heart will shine forth God's mercy and God's forgiveness on all those who seek it.

††††

Chapter 3.

Misunderstanding The Way—
Messages from God, The Father

God, The Father—4/2/95

UNDERSTANDING THE TRUTH

There is only one truth, the truth that comes from God, the truth that is God. Whether or not mankind believes it, it is still the truth.

In times of old many did not believe the world was round, but it is. Many did not believe the earth rotates around the sun, but it does. The truth is the truth, regardless of what mankind thinks. Now understand this truth, in the beginning was God, nothing existed except God. There were no stars, no planets, no gases, no particles, nothing, except God.

God the creator in His love created the first matter and from this matter God made all. It is not important if this matter was minute particles that exploded to create mass, or if it was mass that was brought into being with God's word. All that is of concern is that from nothing God created, and that is the truth whether or not mankind accepts it. Mankind denies so much that is true until it is shown the proof; mankind accepts little until there is evidence to prove it; mankind closes its eyes to the truth until its eyes are opened by overwhelming facts which show what is true.

Now is the time to look at and discuss some of the basic truths which are denied by mankind. Now is the time to open your minds and your hearts to the reality of the true existence of mankind and the universe.

God, The Father—4/2/95

EVOLUTION OF MANKIND

Many say mankind evolved from the apes, if that is so where did the apes come from? The apes are originally descended from fish they say, so where did the fish come from? The fish came from tiny little cells they say, so where did the cells come from? If the cells came from gases, so where did the gas come from?

In the beginning all came from God; it does not matter how certain creatures or plants evolved for they all came from God's love.

Mankind, many scientists say, is a brother to the monkeys. This is true in the sense that God put the animals on earth to be companions, friends, and helpers of mankind. Shouldn't everyone call a companion, a friend, a helper part of his family? Shouldn't everyone treat the animals with love?

Mankind is unique on this planet. It doesn't take much intelligence to see this. If mankind achieved his uniqueness through natural evolution like the animals, then why are there not other species that are achieving similar traits such as reason as they evolve through time? Why, if mankind is descended from apes, have apes not evolved to be more like mankind? Surely they would have to catch up with mankind to some extent for the basic structure, the basic being would be the same and, therefore, with time they should become more and more like mankind. It has not happened and it will not happen because God in His truth did not design it that way.

What God did was to make a paradise for the beings He created in love. He created this paradise with all its plants, its animals, and its beauty so that His children could exist there in love and harmony. God put all that was needed to exist on this planet and

God made it so that all could adapt as the environment changed. God made earth to be a self renewing paradise for mankind.

When earth was ready for His children, God created them to be. God gave them the bodies they needed to exist on this planet and so it is natural that there would be similarities with the animals for they were created to exist in the same environment. Similarity does not mean the same. What God did was to create an image of Himself, which He filled with His love and His spirit. These images were His creation. He called mankind His children, destined to live with God forever in love. These were created by God to enjoy His mercy, His love, and His eternal gift of life. These children created to be with God but not equal with God, these children...God's love.

Mankind, God's gift to Himself, mankind to whom God has given so many gifts. Mankind, a unique creation of God that was made to develop into true spirits of love, spirits of love that no animal will ever be!

God, The Father—4/2/95

THE RELATIONSHIP OF GOD WITH MAN

God, who created mankind, in His wisdom placed mankind above all other creations. God did this so that the gift of an everlasting spirit He had given mankind could develop into the love that it was created to be.

Q. Why didn't God just create mankind as He wanted them to be and not have them develop into them?

A. God in His love enjoys to see His creation of love grow into its true self. It is the same way with a gardener who plants a seed, then watches it as it grows from a seedling to a flower, to show its true beauty. With God He enjoys watching the seed of the Spirit grow and grow until it blooms to become a beautiful flower of love.

Q. Sometimes the spirits of mankind become evil and filled with hate. How can this happen if God created them in love and to be love?

A. When God created mankind and placed him in a paradise where he could grow in love, God also gave man free will. God gave mankind free will to choose an eternity of love or an eternity of darkness. God gave mankind this free will because He loved mankind and did not want to force His will upon them. As with a gardener, God planted the seed and surrounded it with good soil and fertilizer in the form of His love. As with plants some are too weak to grow even though all around them lies the food of life. As with plants, some wither and die due to lack of light and so they shrivel up in the dark.

Q. How can this happen if there is good soil, good food, and good light?

A. When a plant fails to thrive even though it has all the conditions in which it should flourish, then it is because the plant has become ensnared by weeds or attacked by bugs which the plant by itself is not strong enough to overcome. So it is with mankind even though it has all it needs to attain eternal life, sometimes it is not strong enough to overcome the evil that ensnares it and the dark that attacks its very soul. Imagine a garden completely overrun by weeds and insects with only a few flowers struggling through the overgrowth to reach the sunlight. This is how mankind is today.

Q. Should mankind think what would a gardener do in this situation? Should mankind think what will God do in this situation?

A. There is only one solution, and that is to get rid of the weeds and insects, to pull out the withered flowers and to let those who are reaching for the sunlight have freedom to do so.

Q. Although the solution is so obvious, many ask, "Why hasn't it happened before?"

A. God in His mercy and love wants mankind to tidy his own garden and so He sends mankind the means with which to do it. He sends the answer to overcoming the evil and sin on earth that strangles the flowers of love He has created. He sends Himself in His Son Jesus.

Q. Jesus was here nearly two thousand years ago and yet sin and evil are still here. How can that be if He defeated evil?

A. The Lord God Jesus defeated evil with His sacrifice on the cross. The Lord God Jesus saved mankind with His sacrifice on the cross and the Lord God Jesus showed God existed with His sacrifice on the cross.

What Jesus did was to offer salvation to all the flowers in the garden. Sweet Jesus does not want to lose any flower for He treasures them all. Instead of just destroying all that was in the garden that was covered by weeds, He offered those trapped flowers the means to cut themselves free so that they too could see the sun.

This process takes time because the weak and dying need to be strengthened, need to recuperate, and need to be humble enough to accept the help and love offered by Jesus. As these flowers accept God's help, the weeds in the garden try harder to defeat them, sometimes pulling them off course and into the dark part of the garden where they wither and die. What the weeds do not see or understand is that stronger and stronger flowers are growing and shrugging off these clinging weeds. These stronger flowers show that God's love is growing and that one day there will be so many strong and tall flowers of love that all the weeds will fall away and die in their shade.

Sweet Jesus feeds these flowers, nurtures them, prunes them, and directs them to the sunlight. Sweet Jesus plants new seeds in the garden that will grow even stronger and will fill the garden with the aroma of love. Sometime in the future there will be a collecting of the weeds and bugs. They will be put together and will be burnt so that the garden will never again be overrun by evil.

God, The Father—4/4/95

THE RELATIONSHIP BETWEEN MAN AND HIS BROTHERS AND SISTERS

Mankind is increasingly isolated from himself. Instead of growing closer to God, many only see themselves or their immediate family and friends. All else means little.

Q. How has this happened if all were created by God to love and as equals?

A. It has happened because many close their hearts to God and each other. This is how many use the free will God gave them, the free will that was supposed to allow mankind to come to God's glory freely.

Q. Surely then God should take this freedom away?

A. God will not, for He wants the love in man to grow freely not forcibly. What God does do is to show mankind through His Son Jesus, how mankind should live, how mankind, no matter how hard it may be, must love his neighbors, how mankind should share and help each other, how mankind should live in kindness and gentleness and how mankind should be.

Q. It seems not many listen, why is this?

A. Imagine that all mankind was placed in front of a huge mountain of food. That mankind was starving, not having eaten for a long time. Amongst the people there, were some stronger than others and others so weak that they could not move.

The gates in front of the food mountain were opened and the strong started to rush forward leaving the weak behind. The strong ate their fill and then took more in case they might be hungry again. When the weak crawled to the food there was not enough to feed them all. The weak called out to the strong to bring some of the food back but the strong would not as they needed it for the future. Many of the weak died.

Then a voice was heard from the skies saying, "There is enough for all, why do you not share?" The strong replied, "We need to eat tomorrow or we might die then." The voice replied, "There is always tomorrow, who starves then? Eventually the strong will become weak and it will be your turn to starve. Do you think the strong of tomorrow will help you when you are weak?" Some of the strong brought food to the weak and helped them, others decided not to.

The voice said, "I gave you a free choice to help or not to help. Those who have repented and shared will be fed with the living bread from heaven forever. Those who did not, will receive as they have given, nothing."

Those who gave nothing and kept all only see their needs, only consider their hunger because they do not open themselves to love which would show them how precious is each person, how others' needs are as valid as their needs and how by giving and sharing, they will receive in return. The strong are strong so they can help the weak, and the weak are weak so the strong can learn compassion, kindness, and love. They learn by giving.

Q. What of those who do not listen to God, those who only listen to their pride?

A. These children are just as precious to God as those who do lead good lives. Jesus came to save these as well as the good people. Jesus came to save sinners regardless of the amount of sin. Jesus came to bring all home to heaven, all those who would repent and love God. All those who would turn their back on sin and accept the truth.

Q. Isn't it unfair to those who have spent their lives in God's love and service? Doesn't this say, "Well, you can sin as much as you like as long as you repent before you die?"

A. Those who have lived their lives in and for God, would willingly accept their brothers back into God's arms for this is what Jesus taught, He taught forgiveness. Some may, however, because they do not fully understand Jesus' words, feel unfairly treated. This shows that they have not come fully to God. This shows they still put up the barrier of pride that says, "I have been good. I have followed God's word and I deserve more than they." Isn't that greed, not wanting others to be forgiven and share in God's love?

Of course you must lead good and holy lives, of course you must follow God's Son Jesus' word and, of course, you will be rewarded in Heaven. Remember though, God has enough for everyone and the more you give in God's name on earth, the more you will receive in Heaven. God rewards those who do His work, greatly, and God gives glory to His true servants when they come to Heaven. What God also does is love and welcome into Heaven those who truly repent and love God.

This does not mean those who say, "I will sin now and repent later," for this is not true repentance; this is just an excuse to carry on sinning. It may be there is no later, as they may die before they start their so called repentance, then it will be too late. True repentance starts once you are aware you are offending God, you are sinning, for once you know, you are accountable for your actions. Once you know you sin, then you must stop, then you must repent, and then you must lead good lives.

Q. What about people who sin but don't know they are sinning?

A. What it means, is that those who do not know they sin must be told and shown the truth. What it means is that those who have educated others to sin and explained it away with reason will be held accountable for those they have misled. What it means, is that all people have an inner truth that was put there by God and which tells them: "To kill is wrong, to steal is wrong, to lie is wrong," and so much more.

When this inner feeling is ignored, people become uneasy, unwell, and uncomfortable with their actions and this is a sign to stop what they are doing. All people have this, it is just that some people ignore it. When they ignore it and sin, then they are held accountable for their actions.

Q. But these inner feelings don't stop primitive people killing or sinning do they?

A. Primitive people are the same as educated people, some good and some bad. If you look at the various tribes around the world, many live in peace, harmony, and love. This is following their inner gift from God. Others kill, mutilate, hate, and commit so many bad things. Why? For the same reasons as civilized man— greed, envy, anger. So these sin because they do not listen to the inner gift that God has given them.

Q. If Jesus is the way to heaven and non-Christians do not know of Him, how can they reach heaven?

A. First, it is every Christian's duty to make these people aware of Jesus by bringing His love, His words, and His gifts to them. This is a responsibility that must not be ignored, for by this, every Christian can receive graces from God.

Second, if these people died and did not know of Jesus then it is not their fault and this is taken into account by the loving Father in Heaven. This does not mean that they can get to Heaven without Jesus. It means that the Father in His mercy allows them a grace that enables them to accept or deny Jesus as Lord.

The duty of every Christian is to give others the chance to know, accept, and love Jesus before they die. Then, these become living children of God who will defeat evil in their lives and will spread the love of Jesus to others.

Q. What of those throughout the world who will only accept Jesus as human and not divine?

A. These misguided children are being led away from the truth of God by the evil one. These misguided children need to study Holy Scripture and see what it truly says. These misguided children need to remember no one else throughout time has said, "I will die and in three days come to life again," and then fulfilled it.

These misguided children need to understand how many times Jesus showed He was Lord. These misguided children should consider why so many would give their lives so willingly for Jesus.

These misguided children should consider that when they die and they will face Jesus in Heaven, it will be too late then to say, "I believe." All their other so-called gods of money, crystals, cosmic realities, masters of earth, spiritual masters, and masters of evil will not be there to help them. It will be Jesus and the persons face to face. Then who will save them? Then what crystal will protect them? Then what psychic powers will count? As they are judged by the Lord and they see the truth, they will discover the truth is there whether or not they believed it.

†††

Chapter 4.

The Way Home—
Messages from God, The Holy Trinity

God, The Father—10/21/94

Jesus was, is and always will be. Jesus was the Word from the beginning. Jesus is the Word for now and Jesus always will be the Word.

Jesus is love, Jesus is joy, Jesus is happiness. Jesus is My Son, Jesus is Me.

Jesus, Jesus, Jesus. What a song in a name, what love in a name, what God in a name. The one true God. There is a mystery, there is a divine revelation, there is God.

God, The Father—10/21/94

Caring for you, caring for all, caring for souls. Loving you, loving all, loving souls. Protecting you, protecting all, protecting souls. Serving you, serving all, serving God. This is the work of angels.

God, The Father—10/21/94

Pain and sorrow, anger and hate, distrust and cheating, stealing and lying, lusting and killing. All these things man does. All these things come from the dark; yet many embrace them willingly and happily. When the dark beckons, many run to him, many love him, many worship him and many follow him. What silly men!

Love and joy, trust and friendship, truth and honesty, helping and caring, giving and sharing, following God's word and commandments. Not many do these, yet these are all of God. Man runs away from these, man makes excuses not to live this way, The Way. Many follow, but oh, so many more do not. So many reject God and God's love; so many embrace evil and so many spurn good. Is this how mankind is supposed to be? Is this how I wanted man to be? Given a free choice, so many make the wrong one, so many do not know the right one, so many do not know Jesus, The Word. Teach them so they can be saved and come to Me in Heaven. Teach them for Me, in Me, and of Me.

The Holy Spirit—10/21/94

If only all would listen to God. If only. What a world it could be, living and loving in God, with God and for God, what a dream. If mankind could turn and accept love, accept warmth, accept kindness and live to these, then the world would be paradise once more. How can mankind return to love of God? How can mankind remake paradise on earth? How can mankind become what is his true destiny?

Prayer is the only way, prayer is the answer to all, prayer is the gift God gave to men to open the world to Him. Prayer is the way to peace and happiness. Prayers are the words that make the world change. If only mankind would pray more and love more!

†††

Lord Jesus—10/22/94

Violence begets violence, sin begets sin, and love begets love.

God, The Father—10/26/94

Son of Mine as all men are, love of Mine as all men are, friend of Mine as all men should be.

God, The Father—10/26/94

My Son calls to you, My Son waits for you, My Son is next to you. Reach out and feel His love— a love for all. Tell all that it is there for them; they only have to reach out and take it.

God, The Father—10/26/94
        (when the evil one tried to confuse me)

Through the mist of evil, through the veil of tears, and through the sin of man, keep smiling, keep shining, and keep loving.

God, The Father—10/27/94

Mystery, divine mystery. Jesus, divine Jesus. Trinity, divine Trinity. One who is Three and Three who are One.

God, The Father—10/27/94

Sweetness is My Son Jesus. Joy is My Son Jesus. Jesus is for all and all is Jesus. Jesus is for all and all is for Jesus.

God, The Father—10/27/94

Mankind must start to look within.
Mankind must start to look with love.
Mankind must start to look to Jesus.

†††

God, The Father—10/27/94

Show obedience, show respect, show humility in all you do for Me. Live in love, live in truth, and live in Jesus in all you do for Me. Search for God, search for light, and search for Me in all that you do for Me. Stay in God, stay in love, and stay in Me, through My Son Jesus.

Lord Jesus—10/27/94

My dear children, embrace Me in love, embrace Me in joy, embrace Me in the Eucharist. Take Me within and let Me fill you with My love. Take me within and let Me love you completely. Take Me within and love Me.

God, The Father—10/28/94

Loneliness disappears with God in your life, pity for yourself disappears with Jesus in your life, and sadness is gone when the Holy Spirit fills you.

The Holy Spirit—10/28/94

Christians should be happy in Jesus. Christians should be happy in love. Christians should be happy in love with Jesus.

Lord Jesus—10/28/94

Drawing on My love, drawing on My strength, drawing on Me is what you must do in times of trouble and times of trial.

Visions (In Retreat)—10/29/94

I saw a dove over the Eucharist shining a white light onto each person. In the chapel, I saw the crucifix bleeding from the hands and stomach, bright red.

Lord Jesus—10/30/94

Awake in love, awake in joy, awake in Me.
Open to love, open to joy, open to Me.
Wanting My love, wanting My joy, wanting Me.
This is how mankind should be.

God, The Father—10/31/94

Washing your soul in love, washing your soul in eternal love, washing your soul in Jesus. Wringing your soul free of sin, wringing your soul dry of evil, wringing your soul through my Son Jesus. Cleansed with love, cleansed with joy, cleansed with Jesus.

God, The Father—10/31/94

Cling to Jesus, cling to love, cling to Jesus' love.
Cling to Heaven, cling to eternity.
Cling to glory, cling to God, cling to Jesus for He is God's glory.

Lord Jesus—11/1/94

Praising, praying, and thanking is what you must do in good and in bad times. Pray, pray, pray, for help, for love, for Me.

Lord Jesus—11/1/94

Over My people I lay My love, over my people I shower My gifts, and over My people I pour out My mercy.

Lord Jesus—11/3/94

Waiting for My love, waiting for My joy, waiting for Me. You wait in constant expectation for My love, My joy, Me. This is how it should be always, always expect Me, always wait for Me, always love Me.

Lord Jesus—11/3/94

Food of Love, food of Life, food of God, the Eucharist. Feed on My love, feed on My joy, feed on Me, in the Eucharist. Eating of Heaven, eating of Me, eating of Love in the Eucharist.

The Holy Spirit—11/4/94

Yoke of sin, yoke of evil, yoke of pain. Man accepts this yoke and willingly carries its burden. How foolish is man, how naive is man, how silly is man. This yoke only brings eternal darkness, break free from this now and find eternal light through the Lord Jesus.

Vision: Heart covered with a cross—11/4/94

Lord Jesus—11/5/94

Loving others for Me, loving others for you, loving others for them. Loving, loving, loving, do this always, do this freely, do this completely, and do it in Me.

Lord Jesus—11/5/94

Loving you, loving others, loving all is what I do, for I am Love. Embracing you, embracing others, embracing all, is what I do for I am life's embrace.
Comforting you, comforting others, comforting all, is what I do for I am comfort.

†††

The Holy Spirit—11/10/94

A lonely man waits for love, a lonely man waits for friendship, and a lonely man waits for Joy. All men are lonely unless they know Jesus.

The Holy Spirit—11/10/94

Throughout time man seeks God, throughout time man looks for the truth of God, and throughout time man follows the same path. Man only needs to look to Jesus, the answers and the way are there for him.

God, The Father—11/12/94

Praise is for the man who loves God,
Praise is for the man who lives for God,
Praise is for the man who lives by God's law.

God, The Father—11/12/94

One moment is all it takes, a moment in God. One moment is all it needs, a moment in God. One moment is all it requires, a moment in God. To do My work takes but a moment, a moment that is your life. Use this moment for God's glory, My glory. Use this moment for love and use this moment for all mankind.

Visions—11/12/94
Black cross with white edge glistening gold and white. Jesus with gold and white light glistening around Him and dove flying down.

✝✝✝

Lord Jesus—11/12/94

Place your soul in My hands, place your future in My hands, and place your destiny in My hands and live forever.

✝✝✝

God, The Father—11/14/94

Open your eyes, open your heart, open your soul to Me.

Open your eyes and see the wonders I have created in everything around you.

Open your heart and feel the love I have given to all around you.

Open your soul to Me and become part of that creation, that love—Me.

God, The Father—11/14/94

Loving Me is all I ask, loving man is all I demand, loving, loving, loving is living in Me.

ttt

Lord Jesus—11/14/94

Upon a hill stood a cross,
Upon a cross hung a man,
Upon a cross hung God.

The love that was given,
The love that was shared,
The love that was that man, God.

Hanging upon this cross I bore all of man's sins I bore all of man's hatred, greed, lust, anger, fear.

I bore all and I showed that God forgave man all of his mistakes, all of his errors, all of his sins.

I came to forgive, to love and to lead man to his true destiny with the Father.

How it hurts to see man still not believe or understand what God gave to man, what God offered to man, what God still offers man.

How the spear dug deep into My heart, but that is not as deep as the pain man causes Me now with his denying and turning from God.

Each time I see man by his own hand destroy himself, destroy his soul, it tears Me as the nails tore My skin on the cross.

Each time I see man defile his spirit, it cuts Me as the whip cut into My skin.

Each time I see man drink the bitterness of evil, it sours Me as the sponge of hate I tasted on the cross.

Each time I see man pierce his being with the evil one's claws, it reminds Me of the pain when the thorns tore My skin and each time I see man blinded by power, I remember how I was blinded by My blood as it ran into My eyes.

Why does man not understand what he does to himself and what he does to God in Heaven?

Surely man knows what is right and what is wrong, surely mankind can see that the wrong path only causes suffering and pain.

Surely mankind wants to walk the right path.

There is only one right path, the path of love, kindness, gentleness, the path of God.

Place your souls on this · path and place yourselves on the path to eternal joy.

I ask the world to stop hurting itself, to stop torturing its soul, and to start healing itself so that it can walk the right path with Me at its side to guide it along the way.

Lord Jesus—11/15/94

Broken in two, broken apart, broken within.

Broken into two selves, the self of sin and the self of love.

Broken apart, apart from others and broken within your heart, a heart of giving and a heart of taking.

Your self of sin is gone and now only your self of love exists. Your soul is now apart from those you mingled with before.

It is a remade soul.

Your heart is now only for giving, giving to others.

Your heart is now only for taking, taking My love to others.

†††

Lord Jesus—11/15/94

Become one with Me, become one for Me, and become one forever. Link your hand in Mine, link your heart to Mine, and link your soul with Mine.

Lord Jesus—11/15/94

Blood of Jesus, shed for man,
Body of Jesus, broken for man,
Soul of Jesus, love for man.

Lord Jesus—11/15/94

As I walked this earth, I saw and felt what men see and feel. As I walked this earth, I knew what man went through when he faced the evil that exists all around him.

As I walked this earth I chose to endure all the pain that man had within.

After going through all this, I became a true brother to all mankind,

I became one with man,

I became the same man for a moment.

I now look at My brothers and sisters and see and feel all their pain, their suffering and want to lift it from them.

If man would only let Me, I would bring them true comfort, true joy, true happiness.

It is only man that stops this,

It is only man that turns My love into something that is no longer valued.

It is only man who brings the great sadness upon himself.

Take this message to mankind and ask them to open themselves to the truth of God,

Open themselves to the love of God,

Open themselves to Me, Jesus, and be saved.

†††

God, The Father—11/16/94

Taken every day, taken every minute, taken every moment.

This is how My love should be received.

Every day fill yourself with My love.

Every minute live My love and every moment be My love.

My love that is everything for everyone always.

God, The Father—11/17/94

A cross is a gift, a gift to bring you closer to Me.

A cross is to be borne in joy because you share the pain of My Son Jesus.

A cross is to show that you love Me and are prepared to accept all for Me.

A Son of Mine welcomes these crosses as they lift Him to heaven.

Vision—11/18/94—Smell of roses in the car, then Our Lady speaks to me. She tells me she loves me.

Vision—11/18/94—At Mass when saying, "Lord, I am not worthy to receive you," I had a vision of Jesus sitting at a long table with an empty seat next to Him on his right-hand side. He called me to sit and eat with Him and, as I sat down, He held my left hand in His right hand.

After Communion, He appeared again, took my hand and said, "Now you have eaten of Me, walk with Me," and we walked along a path and Jesus said, "Walk with Me always."

Lord Jesus—11/18/94

Eating My flesh, drinking My blood, and walking My way.

What happiness I bring you when you do this and what happiness you bring Me when you do this. Do this always and do it in love.

Lord Jesus—11/18/94

Walking along the way, you will see many wonderful things, walking along the way, you will feel many wonderful feelings, and walking along the way, you will receive many wonderful gifts.

Lord Jesus—11/18/94

I give to you Myself, I give to you My love and I give to you My work. Give yourself to Me, give your love to Me, and give your all for My work.

Lord Jesus—11/18/94

Stars shine brightly, stars shine in the dark and stars shine in the heavens; become a star for Me.

Lord Jesus—11/20/94

King of Glory, King of Joy, King of Love, King of Heaven, King of Comfort,
King of Charity, King of Eternity, King of All, King of Kings, King of Light,
King of Majesty, King of the Eternal Life, King of Mercy, King of Prayer,
King of Suffering, King of Passion, King of Hearts.

†††

God, The Father—11/21/94

The Way is a hard way but it is the only Way.

God, The Father—11/23/94

People are My love,
People are My joy,
People are My children.
My children who should bring Me love and joy,
who should bring each other love and joy, and who
should know they were created for this.

The Holy Spirit—11/23/94

Jesus is the way, Jesus is the only way, for Jesus
is God. The Father gave Himself to man through His
Son Jesus Christ, now man must give himself
through Jesus to the Father. The Father waits for man
to give himself so that He can give man all of His
gifts, all of His graces, all. Mankind only has to
seek them, want them, hunger for them through
the love of God Jesus.

The Holy Spirit—11/24/94

One moment you love Me. One moment you adore
Me, and one moment you are with Me. The moment
is your life, for it is but a moment in eternity.

The Holy Spirit—11/25/94

Always remember to pray, pray in your actions,
words, and thoughts. Pray always and you grow
stronger in Me.

✝✝✝

Lord Jesus—11/25/94 & 12/2/94

Sacraments are special gifts that My Father has
given to mankind to bring them closer to Him.
Sacraments should not be underestimated by mankind.
They should be appreciated for what they truly are,
God's graces to man. Sacraments are especially for

the good of mankind, the good of their souls, their spirits. With the receiving of a sacrament, man gets more than he knows, mankind gets a pure gift of love from God the Father in Heaven. With the receiving of a sacrament, God gives man His love, a love which feeds the soul, which nourishes and replenishes mankind's spirits.

With the receiving of a sacrament, mankind also gives God a gift, the gift that is man accepting God's love, showing God he truly believes and demonstrating man's love of God.

What man must come to understand is the true meaning to each sacrament, the true gift that is there for them, the true love that is waiting for them in each sacrament. Communion with God in the Eucharist is just that, joining with God, becoming one with God through the body and blood of the Lord God Jesus. When Jesus is taken within in this sacrament, He fills your whole being, He fills you with His love, His light, Himself.

It is when the person blocks the love, the light, Jesus Himself, with his disbelief that this truly is the risen Lord's Body and Blood that they do not receive the full benefit that is there for them, the true joy and glory of being one with God. When you receive the Eucharist accept it for what it truly is, Jesus, and allow the Lord to love you completely. Communion should be taken weekly at a minimum and daily as a sign of true love of God.

Confession must be seen for what it is, it is God your Creator cleaning you, forgiving you, making you pure. It is your God saying I love you and I want you to love yourself, I want you to stop hurting yourself with sin. I want you to be the true, pure spirit you were created to be.

It is your God showing His mercy, His kindness, His gentleness, His love. It is your God saying I care for you and so I forgive you.

It is your God saying I love you and I want you to love Me.

It is your God saying be happy, happy by staying in My love, free of sin.

It is your God saying I understand your weakness, your frailty and I still love you.

It is your God saying live in My love and be secure
for eternity. It is your God saying I love you.

Confession is a sacrament that can be taken weekly,
but daily is better.

Lord Jesus—11/26/94

Along the path to God are many obstacles but these
are there so that you can show you truly love and
trust in God. These hurdles are there as steps, steps
you need to take to bring yourself closer to Me, your
God. If you see each one as a challenge, as a battle
of good over evil, then you can overcome them more
easily. I understand how you feel, I know what you
are going through, and I am there for you. Persevere
and become stronger in Me, persevere and become
closer to Me, persevere and become a sign of Mine
to show the way to God.

Lord Jesus—11/26/94

Walking the path is difficult, walking the Way is
hard but coming to Heaven is the reward.

Lord Jesus—11/27/94

Opening your heart to God is opening yourself to
others for God. Opening yourself to God is opening
yourself to love and opening yourself to God's Son
Jesus, is opening yourself to joy. Be open always and
be Mine always.

Lord Jesus—11/27/94

Praise the Lord for His mercy,
Praise the Lord for His love,
Praise the Lord for His joy,
Just praise the Lord for being.

†††

God, The Father—11/28/94

Come to Me in love, come to Me in joy, come to Me in Jesus.

God, The Father—12/5/94

Taking love within, is taking My Son Jesus within. Taking truth within, is taking My Son Jesus within, and taking God within, is taking My Son Jesus within, for He is Love, truth, and God.

God, The Father—12/5/94

Patience is a virtue that all should seek, for patience is needed when seeking Heaven—patience in love, patience in giving, and patience in caring.

Lord Jesus—12/8/94

One man, one Word, one God, Jesus. One year, one day, one moment, redemption. One person, one Spirit, one love, Father.

Lord Jesus—12/8/94

Praise Mother, thank Mother, and love Mother for she loves all mankind; she loves all regardless. Mother just loves as mothers do.

God, The Father—12/8/94

Those who trust in Me will live forever, those who love for Me will love forever, and those who live for Me live in love forever.

God, The Father—12/8/94

Great is the person who lives for God, great is the person who loves for life, and great is the person who lives, loves, and believes in Me, his God.

God, The Father—12/8/94

Slowly turns the world, but quickly goes life;
Slowly turns the tide, but quickly comes eternal life;
Slowly will evil be defeated, but when it happens it will happen quickly.

God, The Father—12/8/94

Truth hurts only when you live in self deception; truth hurts only when you · live in sin. Truth is Jesus and He never hurts, it is only mankind that hurts himself by ignoring the truth.

Lord Jesus—12/9/94

My friends, My love, My joy, this is what all mankind is but many do not accept or believe this.
My love, My joy, and My friendship and all of Me forever.
Mankind should remember this and accept it.

Lord Jesus—12/9/94

Resting in My arms, resting in My love,
Resting in Me is what all souls should do.
Living in My arms, living in My love,
Living in Me is what all souls should be.
Praying in My arms, praying in My love, and
Praying in Me is the way all souls will find the way to the Father.

†††

Lord Jesus—12/9/94

When I look upon My children, I look with love. When I come to My children, I come with love, and when I give Myself to My children, I give with love. Now accept My love and give Me your love. Now accept Me and give Me you. Now accept God and be happy.

The Holy Spirit—12/10/94

Eating with Me is eating of eternal life; drinking of Me is drinking the eternal joy and being one with Me comes from eating and drinking the Body and Blood of Jesus Christ.

The Holy Spirit—12/10/94

In a time of despair the world turns to any solution, it does not think what the final result will be. In a time of fear the world turns to any Savior, it does not look to see who he truly is. In a time of lost faith, the world turns to itself for answers but can never find them.

The Holy Spirit—12/10/94

Let love flow through you, let joy flow through you, and let God flow through you. Open your heart, your soul, yourself to Me, your God; Let Me, the Holy Spirit engulf you with My light, My love, Myself.

The Holy Spirit—12/10/94

One God, one Being, one Love,
One Spirit, one God,
One Father, One Son, one God.

The Holy Spirit—12/10/94

Loving others is a gift, helping others is a joy, and feeling for others a special grace. There is the gift of joy and the grace of a gift.

Our Lady—12/11/94

Opening the door to Heaven is what the Lord Jesus did with His sacrifice. Defeating evil is what the Lord Jesus did with His giving, showing God's mercy is what the Lord Jesus does every time He brings His love to man.

Lord Jesus—12/11/94

Bread of life, food of the soul, Jesus Son of God. Wine of eternal joy, drink of the Spirit, Jesus Son of God.
Flame of hope, fire of love, Jesus Son of God.

God, The Father—12/12/94

Over the cross hung a sign, "King of the Jews." On the cross hung a king, King of Heaven, and in man hangs a cross, a cross of sin, sin which has been crushed by the King but man lets it live on.

God, The Father—12/13/94

Nailed to the cross was man's forgiveness,
Nailed to the cross was man's love,
Nailed to the cross was the Redeemer.
Mankind forgets he has been given these gifts, the gifts of God's love, God's forgiveness, and through God, redemption.

†††

God, The Father—12/13/94

Awaken from your sleep and open your eyes,
Awaken from your despair and open your hearts,
Awaken from darkness and open your spirits.
Open all to God's love, God's forgiveness and God's
redemption.

Lord Jesus—12/13/94

My wounds bleed for mankind,
My heart breaks for mankind,
My spirit weeps for mankind.
Mankind, full of self, full of sin, and full of pride.
Mankind must empty these from self and drink his
fill from My cup, the cup of God's mercy and love.

Vision—12/14/94—Vision during Mass of Eucharist shining with white cross above it.

The Holy Spirit—12/14/94

Cross of strength,
Cross of sorrow,
Cross of forgiveness,
Cross of today,
Cross of tomorrow.

The Holy Spirit—12/14/94

Blood of Christ, divine drink.
Body of Christ, divine meal.
Spirit of Christ, divine light.
Father of Christ, divinity.

God, The Father—12/15/94

Though times are hard,
Though times are tough,
Though times are a struggle,
Always remember God loves you.

The Holy Spirit—12/15/94

Praise God, praise God for His mercy,
Praise God for His love,
Praise God for His glory,
Just praise God.

The Holy Spirit—12/15/94

Make a choice, a choice for good,
Make a choice, a choice for love,
Make a choice, a choice for God,
Just make a choice for the Father.

The Holy Spirit—12/15/94

Holy One, Holy Three, Holy God.
Highest of High, King of Kings.
Spirit of Spirits, Love of Loves,
Joy of Joys, Truth of Truths,
Sacred One, Sacred Three, Sacred God.

Lord Jesus—12/15/94

True love of God is a gift, a gift to you from God
for you to return to God as a gift.
True joy in God is a grace, a grace from God to
you to return to God as a gift when you share it
with others.
True giving is a gift from God to you to return
to God when you give yourself in love to Him.

✝✝✝

101.

Lord Jesus—12/16/94

Turning to God in love,
Turning to God in joy, and
Turning to God in happiness
Is the way to eternal life.

Lord Jesus—12/16/94

Drawing on God's mercy,
Drawing on God's forgiveness, and
Drawing on God's graces,
Mankind can find all of his dreams fulfilled,
All of his prayers answered, and
All of his aspirations achieved.

Lord Jesus—12/16/94

In a time of grace, God shines His love on many,
In a time of mercy, God gives His gifts to many, and
In a time of love, God grows in many.
Not a second passes that is not a time of grace,
mercy and love; God's greatness is always.

Lord Jesus—12/16/94

Three aspects of love, God.
Three views of Heaven, God.
Three hearts that are one, God.

Lord Jesus—12/16/94

Father's love, Jesus' love, Spirit's love;
Father's fire, Jesus' fire, Spirit's fire;
Father's mercy, Jesus' mercy, Spirit's mercy;
Father's joy, Jesus' joy, Spirit's joy;
All the same, all different, all one, all God.

✝✝✝

Lord Jesus—12/16/94

A love of God, a love of man,
A love of truth, a love of goodness,
A love of giving, a love of receiving,
A love of being, a love of becoming one with God.
A love of all things, a love of all people,
A love of helping, a love of healing,
A love of showing the way to Heaven.
A love of praying, a love of the sacraments,
A love of Mary, Mother of God,
A love of Jesus, a love of the Spirit,
A love of the Father, a love of God.
A love worth having, a love worth seeking,
A love there for you and for all,
A love that is life.

Vision—12/17/94—After communion this morning Jesus came to me and said, "Come with Me along this path and see where it leads to."

I went with Him and He took me to Heaven. I saw a large throne with the Father upon it (I could not see His face clearly) with Jesus at His right hand and the Holy Spirit at His left hand. Below Jesus to the right was Mary, Mother of God, and just below her was St. Joseph. To the side of the Holy Spirit and below Him were the three Archangels.

Then below all of them were the Apostles spread out in a straight line with St. Peter first, then below them were millions of Angels and Saints all shining white. All those from Mary down were facing the Father, the Son, and the Holy Spirit saying, "We love You Father, all praise, honor and glory to the Father through the Son and the Holy Spirit."

Everyone turned to me and started to embrace me and say, "We love you." I was filled with joy. The feeling throughout was a feeling of joy, happiness, ecstasy. Then Jesus said to me, "This is what awaits you and all those who follow My path."

Lord Jesus—12/17/94

The merciful Father looks upon His children and says, "To you I send My Son. Rejoice, for God is with you."

The Holy Spirit looks upon His children and says, "To you a child is born, the Child of God, the Son of God. Rejoice, for God is among you."

The Saving Son looks upon His children and says, "To you I come in love and peace, to you I offer salvation. Open your hearts to Me and open yourselves to God."

Lord Jesus—12/17/94

Sanctify yourself in Me, save yourself in Me, lose yourself in Me, find yourself in Me.

Dress yourself in Me, adorn yourself with My gifts, and shower yourself with giving.

True love lasts forever, true hope never dies, and true spirits become one with God.

Trust in Me as I trust in you, love in Me as I love in you, and be in Me as I am in you.

Lord Jesus—12/18/94

Pray for love, pray for joy, pray for Jesus.
Look for love, look for joy, look for Jesus.
Live in love, live in joy, live in Jesus.

The Holy Spirit—12/18/94

Praise the Lord for His mercy, praise the Lord for His grace, praise the Lord for His love, just praise the Lord.

Drinking of the wine, the wine that is Jesus. Eating of the bread, the bread that is Jesus. Becoming one with God through His love, the love that is Jesus.

The Holy Spirit—12/18/94

In a moment, a moment that is your life, you can secure eternity. You can secure it in love or you can secure it in hate, it all depends on how you live now. It all depends on how true your spirit is to its Creator, the Father in Heaven. Over your life you must decide to be in God or to be away from Him, it is your free choice.

Each decision you make in your life becomes a decision for God or against God. Each step you take becomes a step to God or a step from God. Each action becomes an action of God or an action of ignoring God. Each thought can be a thought of God or a thought that takes you away from God.

Each prayer can be a gift to God or can become a thoughtless sentence, a meaningless phrase, a nothing. Each person can become the true spirit God created or can become the dark spirit God despairs over. The choice is yours. Make the right one.

The Holy Spirit—12/18/94

Husband and wife are one to God. Man and woman joined in God's unity, God's love, and God's eyes. Two are one and one becomes two, you for her and she for you. Each half of the whole together one. Love joined never to part, joined to the Father through Jesus' heart. Love of man for woman and woman for man, together they become anointed in Heaven.

Vision—12/18/94—Vision after communion of host shining white with gold and white rays glistening around it.

God, The Father—12/19/94

Playing in love, playing in joy, playing in Jesus is what your soul does each time you pray. When your words of love and praise are received in Heaven they are returned with happiness, a happiness for your soul.

What a gift I give to all of those who pray, they do not understand what they truly receive. They receive My love, My light, Me. They receive fullness of life, they receive true glory. They receive all of My graces, they receive all of My love, they receive Me through My Son Jesus and through My Holy Spirit. What a gift is prayer, what a possession to be sought after, what a joy, what love !

God, The Father—12/19/94

Love is the only truth, God is the only truth, Jesus is the only truth. My Son Jesus is Love, is Truth, and is God.

Lord Jesus—12/19/94

Following My path is a wonderful gift. Along the way are so many opportunities to love, to give, and to be happy. Along this path also lie snares to entrap you, stumbling blocks to trip you, and obstacles to block you. Once you see these for what they are you can overcome them with My love.

God, The Father—12/20/94

Children of the world are children of Heaven.
Children of the world are children of God, and
Children of the world are children of love.
Children of God, children of love,
Children of Jesus, just children.
Children of hope, children of eternal truth,
Children of the Spirit, just innocence.
Children of joy, children of perfection,
Children of God, just love.

God, The Father—12/21/94

Placing trust in Jesus is the most important thing. Putting yourself in the hands of the Redeemer, My

Son Jesus Christ, is the true way to peace and happiness. Joining yourself to Me through Jesus brings eternal joy.

God, The Father—12/21/94

A heart of stone can be moved by love, a heart of ice can be melted by love, and a heart of sin can be cleansed by love, the love that is My Son Jesus Christ.

The Holy Spirit—12/21/94

Opening the soul to God's love is the way man can find eternal happiness.

Opening the soul to God's mercy is the way that man can find eternal joy.

Opening the soul to God's forgiveness is the way man can find eternal peace.

The love, the joy, and the peace that is Jesus.

Vision—12/21/94—Vision at Mass while looking at the Tabernacle—white cloud with chalice and host above it shining.

The Eucharist is your food.
The Eucharist is your love.
The Eucharist is your all.

The Holy Spirit—12/21/94

Acclaim the Lord, praise the Father, revere the Son, and glorify the Holy Spirit.

Sing with the Spirit, sing with the soul, sing with the heart, the joy of loving Jesus.

Shout with the voice, shout with the joy of love, shout with the whole being, the glory of loving Jesus.

Rejoice in love, rejoice in being one with God, rejoice in Jesus. Dance with happiness, dance in ecstasy, dance with Jesus. Walk in love, walk with Jesus, walk to Heaven.

God, The Father—12/22/94

Joy begins and ends in Jesus, life begins and ends in Jesus and hope begins and ends in Jesus. An eternal joy, life, and hope that is Jesus Christ, Son of God.

God, The Father—12/22/94

True ways are the ways of love, true paths are the paths of joy, true steps are the steps of hope. Each step along the path that is the way that leads to Jesus.

Vision—12/23/94—On the plane while praying the Trinity Rosary (33 Our Fathers & 3 Glory Be's)—I had a mind vision. During the 11 Our Fathers, I saw golden rays of light which represented the Father. During the second 11, I saw a golden crown of thorns which was Jesus, and during the third 11, I saw golden flames of the Holy Spirit. A golden ember flew up from the flames and descended into my heart and soul, and became a golden flame within me.

Lord Jesus—12/24/94

A day for sweetness, a day for love,
A day for Jesus.
A day for family, a day for God,
A day for the family of God.
A day for truth, a day for wisdom,
A day for forgiveness, forgiveness in God.
A day for taking, a day for giving,
A day for becoming, becoming one with God.
A day for man, a day for God,
A day for God who is man, Jesus.
Truth of Truths, Love of Loves, Joy of Joys, Jesus.
Son of God, Son of Man, Son of Love, Jesus.

Lord Jesus—(Child)—12/25/94

I love, I love, I love. I love man as he is, I love man how he can be, and I love man for what he will be.
He will be in love with Me forever in Heaven, if he takes My love that is offered to him.

Lord Jesus—12/25/94

Eyes of a mother, eyes of love, eyes of mercy, these are the eyes of Mary, My mother.

Lord Jesus—12/25/94

Cradled in her arms filled with the warmth of her love. Cradled close to her heart feeling each beat of love. Cradled close to her soul, oh so pure and oh so loving.
All mankind can be cradled in Mother's arms and receive the love that awaits them there; all mankind can be guided with motherly care and understanding; all mankind can be children of Mary if they just accept her love and warmth. All mankind can be loved and loved by this Mother of God and this Mother of Man

Lord Jesus—12/25/94

Celebrate today God's gift to the world, celebrate today God's mercy to the world, and celebrate today God's forgiveness to the world. The gift, the mercy, and the forgiveness that are Jesus.

Lord Jesus—12/25/94

Through all the ages I have been loving mankind, through eternity I will love mankind, and throughout time I will wait for mankind's love.

Vision—12/25/94—A vision at Mass of the Baby Jesus naked with white and gold rays streaming from Him.

God, The Father—12/26/94

Turning to God does not mean becoming a fanatic; turning to God does not mean forcing others to your will; turning to God does not mean hurting others. Turning to God means a quiet confident love which you share with others by speaking, giving, loving in the name of Jesus. Turning to God means being one in God's love and being one with your brothers and sisters. Turning to God means shouting God's praises and thanks. Turning to God means peace. Turning to God means denying evil and standing against it. Turning to God means always proclaiming Jesus as Lord.

God, The Father—12/26/94

From the beginning was God, until eternity is God, and forever will be God.

The Holy Spirit—12/27/94

Within the Spirit is love, within the Spirit is hope, and within the Spirit is faith. Just ask the Spirit within and these are all there for you, just ask the Holy Spirit within.

God, The Father—12/28/94

Truth of Truths, My Son Jesus,
Hope of Hope, My Son Jesus,
Faith of Faiths, My Son Jesus,
Love of Loves, My Son Jesus,
Light of Lights, My Son Jesus,
Grace of Graces, My Son Jesus,
God of Gods, My Son Jesus,
God, My Son Jesus.

God, The Father—12/28/94

Just a whiff of happiness, just a glimpse of joy, just a brush with God, this is the time Jesus spent on earth.

God, The Father—12/28/94

From age to age mankind loves Jesus, from dawn to dawn mankind wants Jesus, from second to second mankind needs Jesus, it is just that many do not recognize or understand this. It is just that many deceive themselves and others, it is just that mankind forgets the truth, the truth that is Jesus.

Vision—12/28/94—Today after Mass I stood in front of the statue of St. Theresa in the Cathedral. She started to cry, tears welled in her eyes, and her face was sad. Later, Jesus told me she cried for all the babies killed by abortion.

†††

Lord Jesus—12/28/94

Take a look around and see the love that is wasted.
Take a look around and see the joy that is destroyed.
Take a look around and see the life that is thought
of as worthless. This life is to be joy and love but
it is not given the opportunity to be.

St. Joseph—12/28/94

Become a father, become a son, become a brother
to all.

God, The Father—12/30/94

Walking in love is the way, the love of God,
walking in hope is the way, the hope of God, and
walking in faith is the way, the faith of God. It is
a hard walk but the rewards are great indeed.

Lord Jesus—12/30/94

Jesus watches in love, Jesus waits in love, for
Jesus is Love.

Lord Jesus—12/30/94

Away in a land that is an arid land is a little
town called Bethlehem. This little town was to become
more important than all the cities of the world. Here
in this town was to be born the Light that leads
the way to the Father in Heaven. Here was to be
born the only true Son of God, Jesus.

With the sending of His son to redeem mankind,
God said "I love you and I want to be with you
always." With this special gift of Himself, God showed
mankind how strong was, and is, the bond between
God and mankind. With humility and caring, God's
Son, Jesus, showed how life was to be lived, how
life was to be enjoyed, and how life was meant to

be. It is by following this example that the souls of mankind can return home to God in Heaven. It is by following this example that peace can reign supreme. It is by following this example that all mankind can become true spirits of love. It is by following this example that the spirit of mankind can lift itself in glory to God.

Lord Jesus—12/30/94

Token of Love, token of Joy, token of Grace, My Saints.

Vision—12/30/94—Vision of Mother with a sad face and crying; the statue changed and became shining white. Smell of roses.

Vision—12/31/94—After communion this morning Jesus came to me and said, "Take My hand and walk with Me." He led me through a multitude of red hearts which became roses, then one large red rose.

Our Lord—12/31/94

The end of a year which brought you near,
The start of a walk which led you to God.
The days ahead will bring you to place yourself completely in My love, My love that is Jesus.

Vision—12/31/94—Smell of roses from Our Lady

The Holy Spirit—1/1/95

Happiness in a new beginning, joy in a new start and love in a new time. The beginning of Christ's love, the new start for man in Jesus, and a new time to find God through His Son Jesus Christ.

Holy of Holies, Hosts of Hosts, King of Kings, Jesus in the Eucharist. Son of God, Son of man, Son of Sons, Jesus the Lord.

Sacrifice of Sacrifices, Gift of Gifts, Love of Loves, Jesus on the Cross. Joy of Joys, Ecstasy of Ecstasies, Light of Lights, Jesus in the Resurrection. Love of man, Sacrifice of man, sent for man, Jesus in the Eucharist.

The Holy Spirit—1/1/95

Broken by man, joined by God.
Broken for man, loved by God.
Broken in man, one in God.
Broken for love, resurrected as Love.
Broken on the cross, Regal in Heaven.
Broken of the body, one with the Spirit.
Broken in life, Eternal as God.

Lord Jesus—1/1/95

On a donkey rode the Mother of God, bringing the Redeemer to mankind. On a donkey rode the Savior of mankind, bringing Himself as a sacrifice to God.

The Holy Spirit—1/1/95

The Father and the Son and the Holy Spirit, one in each and three in each.

The Holy Spirit—1/1/95

Placing trust in Me, placing hope in Me, placing you in Me. Place your soul with trust into My hands;

place yourself with hope into My hands; place your spirit into My hands and become your true self.

A mother's day, a mother's feast, a mother's time. Mother of all, Mother of God, Mother of Mothers. A mother's day for all, a mother's time for all and a mother's feast for all to share.

Lord Jesus—1/1/95

Feeling the love of your Mother is such a gift. Feeling the warmth of your Mother is such a joy and feeling the softness of your Mother is such a treasure.

Lord Jesus—1/1/95

Virgin of Virgins, Queen of Queens, Saint of Saints, Mother of God.

Lord Jesus—1/1/95

Rose of Roses, Fragrance of Fragrances and Sweet of Sweets, Mother of God.

God, The Father—1/1/95

Arise and walk in love; arise and walk in peace; arise and walk in joy. The love, peace, and joy that are Jesus.

Awaken the world to My Word; awaken the world to My Son Jesus; awaken the world to My Mercy. The Word, the Son, the Mercy, all the same, all one.

Walk tall in Jesus; walk tall in the Spirit and walk tall for Me, your Father. Walk tall in the one true God.

Speak loudly of love; speak loudly of peace; speak loudly of purity; speak loudly of God.

God, The Father—1/1/95

Run the race until the end; walk the path unto the finish and stroll the way with Jesus, the true Son of God.

The Holy Spirit—1/3/95

A soul can be a symbol of love or a soul can be a sign of hate. The choice belongs to the soul; if the soul takes the wrong path it will live in sorrow forever, in pain forever, but if it takes the right path it will live in love and joy forever.

There is only one right path, the path that is Jesus Christ, true God and true man.

†††

Lord Jesus—1/3/95

Trying to understand the needs of others is a difficult task. Sometimes others do not understand their own needs and they have to be shown with love what they are. Some people do not understand what God asked for when He asked mankind to live in God's love. He asked that you put yourself last and your God first; that you treat others as you wish to be treated. In doing this, you must live completely open to the wishes of your Lord, God.

His wishes are plain to see; they are in Holy Scripture. Follow His word, follow His love, follow Jesus. Jesus said that He would bring His Spirit and His Love into His children but many do not truly believe this and they put their own needs in place of God's Spirit and Love. The mercy of Jesus is timeless and the mercy of Jesus must be proclaimed forever. Jesus who is merciful is also divine and so His Divine Mercy reigns supreme. His truth exists forever and His Word is forever. Following His Divine Mercy is the Truth that the Word is forever. His Divine Mercy is for those in need and that is everyone.

God, The Father—1/4/95

An offering of love, in the temple,
An offering of God, on the cross,
An offering of Christ, in your hearts.
True love suffered for man,
True love sacrificed for man,
True love risen for man.
Time of love, time of joy, time of suffering,
Time of pain, time of hate, time on the cross.
Speaking of love, speaking of joy, speaking of Jesus.

The Holy Spirit—1/5/95

Feel My Love, feel My Joy, feel My Warmth;
The Love, Joy, and Warmth of God.
Seek My Help, seek My Strength, seek My Peace;
The Help, the Strength, and the Peace of God.
Seek My Light, seek My Comfort, and seek My Hope;
The Light, Comfort, and Hope to be found in God.
How do you seek them?
You seek and find them in Jesus. Through Jesus
is the Way to God, for Jesus is one with God. Jesus
is God with the Father and Holy Spirit, so that when
you seek Jesus, you seek the Father and you seek
Me, the Holy Spirit.

The Holy Spirit—1/5/95

Lamb of God, Love of man.
Sacrifice of man, Love of God.

God, The Father—1/7/95

Trusting, trusting, trusting—trusting in love, trusting
in God, trusting in Jesus who is love and who is
God.

Bringing yourself to God, bringing yourself to Love means bringing yourself to Jesus, who is God and who is Love.

Placing yourself in God, placing yourself in love means placing yourself in Jesus who is God and who is Love.

Becoming one in God, becoming one in love means becoming one in Jesus who is God and who is Love.

Making yourself God's, making yourself love means making yourself Jesus' for He is God and He is Love.

The Holy Spirit—1/7/95

Pushing forward for God in love,
Pushing forward for God in giving,
Pushing forward for God in receiving,
Loving all, giving all, and receiving all from God.

God, The Father—1/8/95

Changing in heart and soul, changing in Spirit to become one with Me through My Son Jesus.

Vision—1/8/95—Vision of the Sacred Heart of Jesus and the Immaculate Heart of Mary joining to become one with the thorns interlocked with white roses.

Lord Jesus—1/8/95

Cross of Love, Cross of Justice, Cross of Saving Grace. The Love of mankind that was shown through God's only Son, Jesus. The Justice of Jesus as He forgave man's sins and said, "I love you." The Saving Grace of Jesus as He shed His blood for mankind and held out His heart to everyone.

Lord Jesus—1/8/95

Alone I hung on the cross with My Mother below Me sharing in My suffering and My pain. Throughout this ordeal even when the whip bit deeply into My soul, even when the thorns tore into My skin, into My being. Even when the cross sank into My shoulders and into My heart. Even when the nails drove through My hands and feet, through My spirit. Even as I hung there abused, tasting the bitterness that man had to offer.

Even as the spear opened My body in a final act of taking My dignity. Even through all this I loved man and I forgave him. I still love man and I still forgive him for the giving on the cross was and is forever, the love on the cross was and is forever. I gave and I continue to give. Has man the courage now to accept My gift? Has man the understanding to see what I offer? Has man the strength to accept and in return to be with Me in eternity?

✝✝✝

Lord Jesus—1/9/95

Reaching out to the world in love, extending the hand of friendship, offering My heart and Myself to mankind. What more can I do? Allow Me into you, let Me in and let Me become one with your heart and soul. Together We can spend eternity in happiness with the Father in Heaven. Together We can unite in a marriage of love and together We can become one heart.

Lord Jesus—1/9/95

Drops of blood from My heart fill the chalice of Love. Drops of blood from My heart lift the sin of man from his soul. Drops of blood from My heart bring Me into man's soul. Drops of blood from My heart show the Mercy I have for mankind.

God, The Father—1/10/95

Sign of Love, Fragrance of Joy, My Son, Jesus.
Flower of Heaven, Passion of mankind, My Son, Jesus.
Heavenly Host, Bread of Love, My Son, Jesus.
The Way of Love, the Way of Life, My Son, Jesus.
God in man, and man in God, My Son, Jesus.

God, The Father—1/10/95

Under the shadow of the Cross, stands the whole world.
Under the shadow of Love, stands the whole world.
Under the shadow of Mercy, stands the whole world.
The Love and Mercy shown on the Cross by My Son, Jesus.

Lord Jesus—1/10/95

Praise and prayer, love and joy, Jesus and you.
Praise God and pray for His graces;
Love God and be joyful in prayer.
Jesus is God who loves to hear your joyful prayers.

God, The Father—1/11/95

In a moment your whole life can change. In a moment your soul can change and in a moment your whole being becomes new. This moment is the moment My Son Jesus touches you. This moment is the moment of God's Love and Mercy. This moment is for all who want it. This moment is for all who need it, this moment is for all.

God, The Father—1/11/95

Only when My love, God's love, is accepted unconditionally, only when My Word is accepted completely, and only when My Spirit is accepted

within, can man live his life as he was created to
live.

God, The Father—1/12/95

Truth of Truth is My Son Jesus.
Heart of Hearts is My Son Jesus.
Grace of Graces is My Son Jesus.
Keep Truth in your heart and live in Grace.
Follow the Truth, follow the Light, follow Jesus.
Follow your heart, follow your love, follow Jesus.
Follow God, follow God's Spirit and follow Jesus to
be filled with graces.

Lord Jesus—1/12/95

Inside your hearts, look and see the love that is
there. When you find it, you find Me for I am Love,
a love for all. As I am a love for all, when you
find this treasure within, you must share it with all
you meet. This love is a gift from My Father to you
and it must become a gift from you to the Father
by sharing it with others.

*Vision—1/12/95—At morning Mass when the
Tabernacle opened for communion, Jesus said, "This
is Me opening My heart to My children." I then had
a mind vision of His heart with white beams shining
all around it in the Tabernacle. At three in the
afternoon at perpetual adoration in Midland, the Lord
Jesus moved the Eucharist backwards and forwards
and then side to side in the sign of the cross.*

*When I thought it was my eyes, the Lord moved
it up and down to show me it was Jesus doing it.
This is the second time this happened, as last Saturday
the same thing occurred.*

Lord Jesus—1/13/95

Lying in Love, lying in Grace, lying in Jesus' arms.
Embracing Light, embracing Joy, embracing Jesus.
Living in Love, living in Grace, living in Jesus.
Becoming Light, becoming Joy, becoming one with Jesus.
Shining for Love, shining with Grace, shining in Jesus.
Serving in Love, serving in Joy, serving in Jesus.
Helping with Love, helping with Joy, helping through Jesus.
Guiding in Love, guiding in Joy, guiding to Jesus is your work.

Lord Jesus—1/13/95

Just a walk with Me is all it takes to bring you to Heaven. Along the path there are many obstacles to overcome but if you take My hand and trust Me all will be well. Take My hand now, the hand of Jesus and trust Me. Take My hand now and believe in My way, take My hand now and become My love.

God, The Father—1/14/95

Seeing the changes, seeing the wars, seeing the evil one coming. World of love, world of joy has become a world of hate.

Vision—1/14/95—During "Our Father" at Mass, Jesus and Our Lady held my hands and prayed with me.

God, The Father—1/14/95

Man's foolishness only brings pain,
Man's foolishness only brings suffering,
Man's foolishness only brings sorrow.
The pain, suffering, and sorrow that come from sin only lead to hell.

God, The Father—1/14/95

Mercy is for all who seek it,
Mercy is for all who ask of it,
Mercy is for all those who will accept it.

God, The Father—1/14/95

Merciful Lord, merciful Jesus, merciful Spirit. Three mercies, one mercy.
Merciful Host, merciful Lord, merciful Jesus. One mercy, one God.
Merciful Father, merciful Light, merciful Creator. One mercy, one God.
Merciful Spirit, merciful Grace, merciful Love. One mercy, One God.
Merciful Father, merciful Son, merciful Spirit. One mercy, one God.
Trinity of love, one love. Trinity of God, one God. Trinity of mercy, one mercy.
One love, one God, one mercy, God's mercy.
Three loves, three lights, three mercies, one God.

Lord Jesus—1/15/95

I am in love with mankind, in love with My brothers and sisters, in love with My little ones, in love with all. Are they in love with Me? I know they are, it is they who don't know that they are.

Lord Jesus—1/15/95

Lights of love, jewels of joy, treasures of truth; this is mankind when they accept My Love and My Mercy.

Lord Jesus—1/16/95

Mother of Jesus, Mother of God, Mother of Love.

Lord Jesus—1/16/95

A mother's love is a special love. It is a bond of complete giving, complete loving, complete caring, complete devotion; complete and forever. This is My Mother's love for her children, this is My Mother's love for mankind, this is My Mother's love for all.

Lord Jesus—1/17/95

Drawing on My love, drawing on My strength, drawing on Me. I am waiting to help all those who ask. Just draw on Me and I am there.

Lord Jesus—1/17/95

In a time long ago, came a man who spoke of love, who spoke of faith, who spoke of God. The Father sent this man, the Father sent this love, the Father sent Himself in this man who is His Son Jesus.

The Son shone the love of God on all those who truly sought it. The Son showed all who would see, the love God has for mankind. The Son spoke of God's love to those who would listen.

What a glorious day when the Son showed what God's love could do, what God's love would do to save mankind. What a glorious day when the Son arose to show the world eternal life does exist.

What a glorious day when the Son ascended the stairway of love to Heaven, showing what can be man's if he lives in love, love of God and each other.

What a gift of love when the Holy Spirit came and filled the followers of the Messiah with the Grace of God. What a day, the day the new Church of God was set alight with God's gifts.

When the Mother of Jesus came to Heaven, Mary showed on this day that all can attain this reward of God's love.

When Mother Most Holy was crowned Queen of Heaven, she was crowned Queen of all God's creation and was lifted to her true place in the love of God. Mankind's future is plain to see if he follows the path

of this man Jesus, who is God. He has been told,
he has been shown, and he has been led by Jesus.
All mankind has to do is accept the truth and follow
the way, and an eternal life in God's Glory is his.

Lord Jesus—1/17/95

Rather be in prayer, than in fear.
Better to be in love, than in hate.
Expect to be in battle. than in quiet.
The battle that overcomes fear and hate with prayers
and love.

God, The Father—1/18/95

Faith in My Son, faith in My Spirit and faith in
Me. This is what you need to pray for always for
there will be difficult moments when only faith will
see you through.

God, The Father—1/19/95

Hope of hopes, Strength of strengths, Love of loves.
Jesus, My Son.
Light of lights, Truth of truths, Mercy of mercies.
Jesus, My Son.
Sacrifice of sacrifices, Savior of Saviors, Son of Sons.
My Son, Jesus.

Lord Jesus—1/19/95

Tasting sweetness, tasting love, tasting happiness,
when you receive Me in the Eucharist.
Love of man, love for man, love in the Eucharist.
A man can find joy, a man can find love, a man
can find Me in the Eucharist.

God, The Father—1/20/95

Dove of Peace, Spirit of Freedom, Father of Love. The Peace, Freedom, and Love to be found in God. Running on love is what you must do, for love is your fuel, your energy. Where do you find love? Only in the Eucharist.

God, The Father—1/20/95

God of Mercy, God of Love, God of Forgiveness, God of All.
God of Graces, God of Gifts, God of Giving, God of All.
God of Goodness, God of Joy, God of Eternal Happiness, God of All.

God, The Father—1/20/95

Faith in God is love of God, and love of God is faith in God.

God, The Father—1/20/95

Aroma of Love is the Breath of Jesus, Dew of Mercy is the Blood of Jesus, Flower of Paradise is the Body of Jesus. All are to be found in the Eucharist, for the Eucharist is Jesus.

God, The Father—1/20/95

Under the cross was a pool of blood which mingled with the earth that lay there. Jesus' blood became one with the earth and one with man. This mingling of blood and earth was a sign that Jesus, My Son, loved mankind. This mingling of blood and earth said that all of this planet belonged to God. This mingling of blood and earth became the joining of Heaven and earth. This mingling of blood and earth became the stairway to Heaven. This mingling of blood and earth said, "You are Mine." This mingling of blood and earth said, "Accept My Love."

This mingling of blood and earth said, "Death is but a door to eternal life with God." This mingling of blood and earth said, "I give Myself, now give Me yourselves." This mingling of blood and earth said, "I love you forever."

God, The Father—1/20/95

Faith in Jesus' saving love will see you through, prayer in Jesus' saving grace will overcome, and trust in Jesus' mercy will lift you to Heaven. Jesus' Love is a Saving Grace given with Mercy.

God, The Father—1/20/95

Fruit of Love, Fruit of Joy, Fruit of Happiness, Fruit of Jesus.

Food of Love, Food of Joy, Food of Happiness, Food of Jesus.

Flower of Love, Flower of Joy, Flower of Happiness, Flower of Jesus.

Lord Jesus—1/21/95

In a time of difficulties, just turn to Me for I long to help. In a time of confusion, just turn to Me for I give you My peace. In a time of uncertainty, just turn to Me and I will strengthen you. Just turn to Me in prayer and I am there.

Lord Jesus—1/21/95

Love is a two way street. I bring you My love and you bring Me your love and when our love meets, it is a joining together to become one in Me.

Lord Jesus—1/21/95

Restless in love are those who do not appreciate its true value.

Restless within are those who do not understand what love really is.

Restless in spirit are those who do not see what is awaiting them in love; it is I, for I am Love.

Lord Jesus—1/21/95

Simple messages, direct messages, clear messages, repeated over and over until mankind comes to Me. Clever arguments mean nothing, intelligent words are nought, superior translations are wasted if the love of God is not within. Be simple in My love, be pure in My love, and be truthful in My love.

Do not try to be what you are not, do not try to win arguments with intelligence, just show your love of Me and your faith in Me and you will win for Me. Nothing else matters except your trust in Me, your love of Me, your faith in Me, and your service for Me.

Lord Jesus—1/22/95

Living through times of pain is hard, even the smallest rejection from a loved one can hurt deeply. Imagine how I feel as I am continually rejected by My loved ones.

Forgiveness is part of loving so always forgive and always love.

Lord Jesus—1/22/95

When times are lonely, I am there. When times are sad, I am there. When times are oh so quiet, I am there. I am the lover of the lonely, I am the Savior of the sad, I am the friend of the quiet times.

✝✝✝

Lord Jesus—1/23/95

In times of fun, in times of enjoyment, and in times of love, think of Me for I am enjoying the fun of loving with you.

Lord Jesus—1/23/95

A momentary thing is life, an eternal gift is love, so find eternal life in love.

A momentary thing is life, an eternal gift is light, so find eternal life in light.

A momentary thing is life, an eternal gift is forgiveness, so find eternal life in forgiveness.

I am Love, I am Light, and I am Forgiveness, so find Eternity in Me, your friend Jesus.

The Holy Spirit—1/25/95

Men of wisdom see beyond the surface and see the truth.

Men of wisdom see the truth that is in the Word, the Word that is Jesus.

Men of false wisdom see only the surface and the glory for themselves; in their wisdom that is really foolishness.

Men of false wisdom are only deceiving themselves and following the path to destruction.

The Holy Spirit—1/25/95

Waiting on each word, waiting on each thought, waiting on each action. The words of love, the thoughts of love, and the actions with love that bring you closer to Jesus

God, The Father—1/26/95

Loving, in times of difficulties is hard, but this is when you show your love is true.

Smiling, in times of hardship is difficult, but this is when you show your true self.

Giving, in times of struggle is difficult, but this is when you show your love of God.

Lord Jesus—1/26/95

A step along the path to Heaven is never easy... each step is a struggle with yourself, and each step is a fight with evil.

When you overcome yourself you overcome evil, when you overcome your weakness you overcome evil, and when you overcome your sin, you overcome evil. Then the steps to Heaven become clearer, simpler, and easier to follow, but still hard to walk.

God, The Father—1/27/95

Everything was created from My love, through My love, for My love and to become My love. Everything from the smallest to the largest is an expression of My love. All things came from My pure love and light and were created to magnify this love, this love which is God.

As everything in creation is of love, then it can only grow in love. Love is the food, the energy, the force that keeps creation alive. Love is the only necessity for life for it is in love that all exist. My Son Jesus is that love, My Son Jesus is that light, and My Son Jesus is the only way to live life eternal.

Mankind came from My love and exists of My love, therefore, the only way mankind can return to Me in Heaven is by love. Nothing that is not love can exist in Heaven, nothing that denies love can reach Heaven, and nothing that lets love out of its spirit can become one with Me in Eternity.

When mankind does not live in love, which is needed for its very existence, then it cannot exist.

When mankind does not live in love, then it cannot grow. When mankind does not live for love, then it cannot come to Heaven and claim its true inheritance in Eternity.

As love is man's food, man must eat of it.

As love is man's energy, man must fill his being with it.

As love is man's force, to exist, he must accept it.

As love is Jesus, man must eat of Jesus,

As love is Jesus, man must fill his being with Jesus,

And as love is man's force to exist by, he must exist in Jesus.

God, The Father—1/27/95

Everlasting love, everlasting joy, everlasting life in the Eucharist.

Everlasting hope, everlasting grace, everlasting glory in the Eucharist.

Everlasting strength, everlasting power, everlasting truth in the Eucharist.

Everlasting, the Eucharist.

The Holy Spirit—1/27/95

Young in love, young in joy, young in truth. Stay pure as the young, be sweet as the young, and be as innocent as the young, and then you are close to God.

Vision—1/28/95—At Mass this morning, a vision of Jesus holding my heart in His hands and setting it alight in the flames of the Spirit.

At communion these words by Jesus: "Peace of Peace, Joy of Joys, Love of Loves, the Eucharist."

The Holy Spirit—1/28/95—(For prayer meetings)

My children, the path ahead is filled with traps and snares to lead you away from My work. See the love of Jesus always and follow that, for it is this that will see you through.

This moment is a special moment, for now you lay out the path that leads many to Heaven. You now embark on an important task, the task of saving souls, the work as followers of Jesus Christ for which you are here. This day, as you sit here, is a day all of Heaven rejoices over this day God smiles on you. Spreading God's Word, spreading God's love, and spreading God's forgiveness is the way ahead.

The gifted among you must use their gifts to glorify God. The gifted among you must spread the healing touch of Jesus to all. Know that I give My gifts so that they are used to bring My children back to Me. Know that I choose those who do My work, regardless of the obstacles placed in their path.

You now have the work of God to do; you now have the love of God to spread; you now have the light of God shining on you. March forward in glory for God, march forward in love of God, and march forward in truth for God. Do not be taken from My path, do not be weakened by those who, in a good heart, oppose My chosen because they do not understand or believe. Do not forget to look at the words, the deeds, and the love, and then you will know you do God's work.

Embrace this task and take My love into your hearts, and you will see the path clearly ahead. The gifts I have given are to be used; do not waste them. Mould yourselves into a team of God's servants with only God's glory as your aim. The world awaits—the gifts are here—take them and show My love to all; the people stray—lead them back with My Words; the children are lost—find them in My name.

God, The Father—1/29/95

A man must find himself in Jesus, a man must find everything in Jesus, and a man must trust in Jesus. Finding himself while looking for everything, brings him to trust Jesus.

Lord Jesus—1/29/95

Roaming through the recesses of your heart you will find Me there. I am only hidden by your thoughts and by your doubts. If you open your heart and believe, then I am there waiting to love you. Open your heart, open your soul, open your spirit and I am there loving you. Open yourself in prayer and invite Me into your life.

Lord Jesus—1/29/95

As I hang on the cross throughout eternity I feel the pain of man's sins. I hang there in love exposing My heart to man saying "I give you My all, I give you My love, I give you Me." I hang on the cross waiting to hear the words of love returned to Me by mankind. I hang on the cross with the nails tearing into My soul, tearing into My love, tearing into Me. Each nail reminds man what his sins have cost and how much I love him. The thorns in My crown bite into My skin and each thorn reminds man how I long for him to be with Me in love.

133.

God, The Father—1/29/95

Running to the beat of My Son's heart is the only race to run.
Racing to the love of My Son is the only way to run.

God, The Father—1/29/95

Jesus opened His arms on the cross and embraced mankind with His love.

God, The Father—1/29/95

Faith in God, love of God, and hope through God is the only way to Heaven.

God, The Father—1/31/95

Those who have God's work to do, must become strong in prayer and weak in themselves, strong in Jesus and weak in the world, strong in faith and weak in self, strong in truth and weak in pride.
Those who have God's work to do, must become pure in love.
Those who have God's work to do, must follow Jesus and by following Jesus lead others to Him.
Loving all for God is a gift, leading many to God is a grace, and learning to accept this gift and this grace, is learning to love.

God, The Father—1/31/95

Whenever times are sad, whenever times are low, whenever times are empty, just think of Jesus.
Whenever the day is full of suffering, whenever the day is full of pain, whenever the day is full of despair, just think of Jesus.
Whenever you feel lonely, whenever you feel lost, whenever you feel down, just think of Jesus.

The Holy Spirit—1/31/95

Love sweet Love, Jesus sweet Jesus, God sweet God.

Truth only Truth, Grace only Grace, Jesus only Jesus.

Faith true Faith, Hope true Hope, Jesus true God.

Lord Jesus—1/31/95

Precious Blood, sweet Body in the Bread of Life.
Love of God, Light of God in the Bread of Life.
Mercy of God, magnificence of God in the Bread of Life.

The bread that is My Body.

Vision—1/31/95—Vision after Mass of bed of roses with Jesus' Heart in the middle saying "Love, Eternal Love." Jesus said, "I give you My Heart."

Lord Jesus—1/31/95

Asleep in the arms of Mother, resting in her warmth, her love. Each breath gently rocking Me into sleep full of bliss, each beat of Mother's heart reverberating through Me and filling Me with her love. Every moment a moment of deep fulfilling joy, every second a second to treasure. Mother's love rocking Me to sleep in the depths of My soul. Mother's love tenderly caressing My spirit, as only true love can.

God, The Father—2/2/95

My children, I am in the deepest of loves with you. I long for you to open your hearts to Me completely. Open them without any barriers, just accept My love, accept My gifts, accept Me. To do this you must give yourself completely to Me, be one with Me in love.

This is hard to do but if you try, the rewards are great. I know many try hard to follow My Word and to live My way and often stumble along the path. Do not worry, keep trying, persevere and you will reach My love.

My Son Jesus is waiting to help you in your difficult moments, just ask and He is there. Strengthen yourselves in prayer and the path will be easier to follow. Now reach out and take My love and come to Me in glory.

Vision—2/2/95—Vision during sorrowful mysteries of Jesus with crown of thorns. I felt so sad tears welled in my eyes. Later during glorious mysteries vision of Jesus ascending into heaven with blood dripping from His wounds. On each drop was written 'LOVE.'

Lord Jesus—2/2/95

Father of Love, Father of Joy, Father of All, Father in Heaven.

Creator of All, Creator of Joy, Creator of Love, Father in Heaven.

Lord of Love, Lord of Joy, Lord of All, Father in Heaven.

Father's Love is so deep, you cannot fathom it,
Father's Love is so strong, you cannot overcome it,
and Father's Peace is so calm, you cannot disturb it.

Lord Jesus—2/2/95

A father looks upon his children and sees so much hope in them for the future. A father looks upon his children and waits to help them achieve their full potential. A father looks upon his children and wants to give them all that is in his power to do. A father looks upon his children and wants to celebrate in love with them, all their successes, and wants to comfort them in love for all their failures.

A father looks upon his children and sees himself in them. A father looks upon his children and sees what can be. A father looks upon his children and just wants to love them and help them. This is how it is with the Father in Heaven, as He looks upon all His children on earth.

Lord Jesus—2/2/95

Spending time alone with Me is the way to come closer to Me. Sitting in My Father's house and just being with Me fills you with My Spirit. Opening your inner self to Me in our time alone accepts My love into your heart.

True friends long to be together, true brothers long to share with each other, and true spirits long to be filled with love. I am Love and I long to fill you.

Part III

The Way Of Life

Chapters: Page:

1. The People—   138.
      Messages from God, The Son

2. The Sacraments—   157.
      Messages from God, The Son

3. The Church—   163.
      Messages from God, The Son

4. The Advice—   166.
      Messages from God, The Holy Trinity
      and from Our Lady

Chapter 1.

The People—
Messages from God, The Son

Lord Jesus—7/22/95

Once there was a bond between God and man that joined them in love. That bond has been broken many times by man but God keeps offering it over and over to mankind.

When mankind first broke this bond, original sin was committed. Each time mankind breaks the bond, it is always when the same sin is committed. The sin is the sin of pride; it was pride that took man from Eden and it is pride that causes mankind to commit so many other sins.

Pride is the core of all mankind's problems. It is pride that says, "There is no God." It is pride that says, "I am master of all." It is pride that says, "I can do what I want; it is up to me." It is pride that says, "Others are inferior." It is pride that says, "I must have more." It is pride that says, "Life is not important." It is pride that says, "We can force our will upon others." It is pride that says, "Mankind is its own master and answers to no one."

Mankind needs to look and see what pride has cost him, what his pride has taken away from him. Look and see how many are happy and content in the world, not many. Most are suffering either emotionally, physically, or spiritually. With this suffering comes the sorrow in the world, the suffering that could so simply be avoided. There is no need for anyone to be lost in this world, no need for any pain or suffering. Everything has been offered to mankind so that he could live. Everything is there for mankind, he just has to want it and accept it. Everything awaits mankind if he will only ask for it, but in the asking, accept in humility what mankind's real life should be.

It is in humility that all will be possible, for when you are humble you show how you love and care for others. In humility, you show that you want everyone to live a life that is happy and content. In humility, mankind will find the true peace and comfort that comes from sharing with his brothers and sisters. In humility, none would be allowed to starve, none would be inferior, none would be unwanted, none would be unloved. Humility, the opposite to pride, with the opposite results. Humility, a joy for mankind; pride, a heavy stone for mankind.

Lord Jesus—7/23/95

There is an inner feeling in man that tells him that his behavior is wrong but mankind smothers this feeling with pride. When humility is embraced, this feeling comes so much clearer and guides each individual down the right path.

This feeling is a gift from God that was given so mankind could live the way he was created to live. This feeling is often called conscience, a conscience that the animals do not have, but mankind was given in love by God so that he could become the true spirit that he was created to be.

God gave man a conscience so that the path to Heaven would be easier to follow. God gave mankind a conscience so that all would live in love. God gave man a conscience as a gift of love, a gift which many turn their backs on, many reject, and many ignore.

Mankind, created from God's love to live in love; mankind of whom most reject God's love, and replace it with love of self. This love of self is what keeps mankind struggling in pain and suffering. It is obvious, but mankind's pride blinds him to the obvious, deafens him to the truth, and closes his heart to God.

When God in His mercy and grace sent His Son Jesus to earth, God sent Him to reawaken these hidden feelings, to reawaken the true love of God, and to reawaken the love and respect of each other.

The words Jesus spoke were all spoken in love, of love, and for love. Jesus came and said to mankind be gentle, be caring, be kind, be humble, be loving, be truthful, and be in love with God.

Jesus came and showed that even though He was, is, and always will be the true Son of God, He remained humble. In His humility, Jesus showed how life was meant to be. Jesus talked only of love for He is Love. Jesus showed only love for He is Love.

If mankind can follow the map of life that Jesus drew for them, so it would be easier for each soul to find his way home to Heaven, then evil will disappear from this planet and it will become the Garden of Eden once more.

Lord Jesus—8/4/95

Within the heart of Jesus is a special place for each person, a unique place that is there for everyone. Jesus wants all to come and claim this place and to unite with Him in eternal joy and love. With this in mind the Lord offers all of mankind the opportunity to love Him.

He knows how difficult it is for some to accept His love, difficult because of the pride that may block it, difficult because of the feelings of unworthiness, difficult because of the embarrassment that may come with accepting the Lord's love, difficult because of the disbelief that Jesus is Lord, difficult because of the evil that has confused and engulfed mankind.

What Jesus says is, "Listen to My advice and heed it, for I give it in love and to help." This is the advice of Jesus Christ, your Redeemer, your Savior, your God who loves you and longs for your love.

Look within and see how you really are, do not look with blurred vision, look truthfully at yourself and your life. Look and see. Have you lived for self, not others? Have you put yourself above others? Look and see if you have mistreated others, been unkind to others. Have you lied, stolen, swindled, cheated, used others for your desires without truly considering their needs? Have you hurt others physically or emotionally? Have you spoken unkind words about others? Have you embarrassed others or humiliated others? Have you done any of these? Most have at some time in their life, for this is part of being human, these things are part of the weakness that is in mankind since he first sinned.

Does your pride stop you admitting what you have done or does it make reasonable excuses for these actions? This is how pride works; it covers up that which is harmful or wrong with reasons that make them seem acceptable.

What many need to do now is to look within with humility, see their faults, the mistakes they have made in life. See how they have hurt others and themselves, see these things, repent and change. Promise to try not to repeat their mistakes, their sins and try to live a life of sharing and caring. It is in this way that mankind can overcome the pain and suffering he accepts and welcomes.

Lord Jesus—8/12/95

Try as it may, mankind cannot overcome the basic flaw in his character, the flaw that is original sin. With this inability comes an acceptance that says it is part of mankind, it has always been this way, it will never change. How clever is the evil one to have convinced mankind this is so.

With this acceptance, mankind allows more and more wrongs, allows sin, more evil. Does not the world understand that it can overcome sin? It can defeat evil, it can live as it was created to be. To overcome the evil that abounds, all mankind has to do is accept Jesus' saving grace, this is the true acceptance that mankind should welcome, not reject.

When a grace is offered, it should be accepted for it is offered for mankind's benefit, not harm. When a grace is offered it should be seen for what it is, it is God saying, "I love you and I want to share My love with you." When a grace is offered, it should be sought after as the true treasure of life, not spurned as useless.

With time, the true saving grace that God offered on the cross has by many been ignored, rejected, scoffed at, and abused. The suffering Jesus accepted to free mankind from his sins is often seen as worthless or as a fictional story made up to make man act better. It is not seen for what it truly is, the victory of good over evil.

It is God saying to mankind that evil cannot harm you if you deny it, that God will protect you. It is God saying that life on earth is not the great prize but it is eternal life in heaven that is to be treasured. It is God saying that what may seem like defeat is really victory that has freed all, if only they will accept it. It is God saying, "I love mankind so much I will endure pain, suffering, and death so that My children can be happy." It is God saying, "Come to Me and be happy."

Lord Jesus—8/20/95

What mankind has forgotten is how to love God. Some love God but most do not, most love other gods, gods of self, gods of sin, gods of the dark. Most do not seem to understand how to live in God's love, they only seem to understand how to live away from God.

Reasons are made for not loving God, reasons are made for ignoring mankind's loving Creator. Some reasons are so wrong that even a child could see they are wrong. What happens when people do see the mistakes, the wrongs, the errors is that these people are considered extreme, mad, fanatic, or just unusual.

The wrongs are seen as the rights by most and anyone who opposes the rights are to be pitied, abused, or scorned. Again you can see that mankind's sin of pride is at work once more, pride that says, "I am right, what I do is all right, I know what is best, God wouldn't expect me to be any other way because I understand what God says." Isn't this the pride that has been with mankind from the beginning? The pride of original sin?

Mankind in his pride looks at himself and says, "We are masters of all, we can unlock the answers to all, we can be as gods." What foolish children to think this way, what foolish children for following this path, the path that only leads away from God, the path of self destruction.

Why does mankind want to be master of all, what good will it do if he has lost love? Why does mankind want the answers to all, what good will it do if he cannot use them in love? Why does mankind want to be God's equal when he can live in God's love eternally and be happy forever? Mankind has lost so much because he looks for more. Mankind has given away the most wonderful treasure of all for the sake of what he may have or what he may find. Mankind only needs to understand that he has everything there...everything awaits mankind in God's love.

What turns people to their so-called gods? When all the one true God offers is love, joy, and happiness, what makes mankind search for more? Surely that is enough? What do these other gods, which are really deceptions, offer mankind that they take him away from the true God? Usually it is power, wealth, glory.

Often it is to do what you want for your own gratification, regardless of others; sometimes, it is pressure to be as everyone else so as not to be abused. All these things are things of self whether it be the self of greed, the self of lust, the self of power, or it is in one's weakness that these are accepted.

Mankind, still searching, but searching in the name of self not in the name of love, still searching in weakness instead of in the strength of God. Mankind lost along the way but blind to his predicament.

That moment when mankind understands what he does to himself and what he does to God who only loves him, will be one of the saddest and yet one of the sweetest moments of existence.

It will be sad because the realization of the pain and the suffering that mankind brought upon himself by accepting sin, realizing it could all have been avoided, then coming to terms with the pain that God has had to bear on the cross because of mankind's weaknesses. Seeing how much the God of creation has had to put up with because of His reckless children will be enough by itself to break mankind's heart.

It is at this moment that the sweetest joy will be there because then nearly all will seek forgiveness, nearly all will want to return to God, nearly all will reject evil, all except those who are so deep in sin that they cannot and will not accept the truth, the truth of God.

What a wonderful moment this will be when the children turn to the Father through Jesus, with the grace of the Holy Spirit and ask to return to the family of God. The lost children returning, the prodigal sons coming home, what celebrations there will be in Heaven and on earth. What happiness will be there for all who are returning to God, what joy, what love.

This is what God longs for. This is what God wants for His children. This is the moment the whole of creation waits for, the moment of love.

Lord Jesus—8/21/95

In love, mankind will find all his needs fulfilled, in love, mankind will see that being humble is a special gift that God gives and God treasures. In love, mankind will come to understand the true value of life, the true meaning of life and the true existence that awaits all. It is love that opens mankind to God and it is love that leads mankind to Heaven. Love is sometimes misunderstood, sometimes not recognized for what it truly is and not given the true value it has.

Love is so special, it is everywhere, it is everything, it is the air you breathe, the water you drink, the food you eat, the animals with which you exist side by side, the plants, the trees, the very planet you stand on, the universe in which you exist. Love is everywhere, it is only that mankind often does not recognize it.

All these things have been created by God's love, of love and with love. They have been created to exist in harmony, the harmony of God's love. Every time you breathe, you breathe in God's creation of love. Every time you eat, you eat God's creation of love. Every time you look upon an object, you see an object of God's love. Everything created in love to be love and to live by love. Everything created pure and wonderful, everything beautiful in its own way. Everything a gift of love from God.

When mankind tries to create, he often creates without love and the results are there for all to see. The air is polluted, the water is fouled, the animals die, and mankind destroys himself. If only mankind would open his eyes and see that anything that is not created of God's love only destroys, only injures, and eventually cannot exist. This is what is happening in the world today, this is what is destroying the earth, killing the animals, and wounding mankind's soul.

It is so clear that only goodness can exist in goodness, anything else must die. Think of a fish created to live in water and to survive only in water. Take the fish from the water and eventually it dies, it may struggle and gasp for a while but without water it cannot exist for long. It is the same for mankind, created to live in love and to survive only in love. Once mankind starts to live outside love he brings his own destruction upon himself. Look now at the state of the world and see the fish struggling and gasping, this is how mankind is because of all the sin and evil in the world. Eventually the struggling will stop, for some it will stop because they stay out of the love of God and for others it will stop because they return to the love of God. The choices are free choices, struggle and die out of love or live forever in love, the love that is needed for your very existence, God's love.

Love as you can see is more than a warm feeling, more than a word, more than a sweetheart's embrace. Love is there for all, needed by all but misunderstood by most.

Love comes down to choice, for if there were no free choice there would be no love. Love is offering the freedom to return that love or to deny it. Love is taking the pain with the joy, the pain of rejection and the joy of acceptance. Love is there for all but it is up to all to accept it.

A look at the results of mankind's history shows and confirms the disasters and evils that come from living away from God.

If you look back at the history of mankind you can clearly see that whenever evil is strong, wars, murder, rape, and so many bad things happen. Whenever did a true man of God start a war, whenever did a true child of God commit evil? Sometimes however, wars and evil are given the semblance of respect, of being God's willl, but it is mankind that does this, not God. Throughout history many good people have fought for God, have killed in God's name, this truly is a misunderstanding of God's will for did not God say in His commandments "Thou shalt not kill?" This again is a sign that mankind does not understand what God asks of him. This again shows that mankind in times of struggle does not put his complete faith in God.

The times when mankind needs to trust in God seem to be the times he turns away. Trust in God would bring peace to the world, would end wars, would defeat evil, trust in God would answer all.

Look today at the countries that were under the yoke of communism. They were not freed by force of arms, Russia became free by the many prayers sent to God for its freedom. It took many years but it happened, imagine how much more would happen if the world united in prayer. Russia in its freedom is now confused and lost; it needs guidance along the path to true happiness.

This can be achieved if those who love God continue to pray for its return to God's family. Evil now tries to take Russia away, it tries to stop its return to the fold, it tries every means possible to keep this great land and great people from God's love. Prayer is needed around the world to defeat this evil, only half the battle was won with the defeat of communism, the battle continues now, and so prayer for Russia must continue.

Prayer is the strongest weapon against evil that mankind has at its disposal. Why is it that weapons of mass destruction are grasped at eagerly, but the true weapon of love in prayer is often ignored? If evil is to be defeated it must be defeated with goodness, not evil, for what victory is that? If goodness turns to evil for help, then it is evil that wins no matter how it may appear at the time. It becomes another victory for evil, another taking man away from God. How cunning is evil to get those who come in goodness to use evil as their weapon to defeat evil, what a hollow victory!

Peace and tranquillity only come from goodness. When evil is embraced, chaos and confusion reign. The world today is in chaos, is confused, so many wars, so much crime, so much evil. Surely this says to mankind something is wrong, surely this says your ways have failed, your successes are outweighed by your failures and what successes you do have are often turned into instruments of the dark. How many advances have been made in technology only to be used for weapons of destruction?

The advances mankind should seek are the ones that bring the family of mankind together, the advances that lift poverty, hunger, violence, and crime.

The advances that mankind should make are advances in love, in life, in liberty. The advances that bring him closer to God, closer to eternal joy, closer to Heaven.

To advance should mean to love.

To advance should mean to care.

To advance should mean to be gentle.

Any other advance is really a step backwards,

Any other advance is a deception,

Any other advance is a path that leads from God.

Lord Jesus—8/26/95

To look at the way mankind lives, how mankind exists, it breaks the heart of God to see how such a miracle of creation that is mankind, can turn from what is good and embrace what is bad. The Father in His mercy opens His heart to His children and welcomes them home; it is only up to mankind to accept the mercy that is offered.

When you look at the way mankind exists, in so much pain, so much sin, when you see the struggle of so many to survive, to find a meal, to find a job, to find love, how can anyone think the world is a good place to be in? No matter how you live, how comfortable your life may be, when others are suffering, the world is not a good place.

†††

When you sit by idly enjoying your wealth, your security and others have nothing, you participate in sin. Your inaction is the same as turning your back on a drowning man and letting him drown; you may not have killed him but by your inaction you have contributed to his death.

Now is the time for mankind to shake himself out of the sleep he has been in for a long time. Now is the time for mankind to open his eyes and his heart. Now is the time for mankind to say no to evil, and yes to God. Now is the time for mankind to show his true self, the self of goodness, the self of compassion, the self of mercy, and the self of helping others. Now mankind can arise from the bed of sin he lies in and show his true self in the glory of God's love.

Mankind must surely see for himself that life cannot go on as it is, that there must come a point of no return where everything will be lost, where all will be destroyed. Before it is too late, mankind has an opportunity to change, a change for the better, yet it seems to frighten so many or seems impossible to others.

Mankind can change; it only needs the will to do so. Mankind can exist in goodness and love, it only has to want to do so. Mankind can become happy and joyful in God and each other again, it only has to try. God waits to help His children change, they only have to make the choice themselves. God knows it will not be easy at first, and so He has many gifts and graces to give to help the world change. They just need to be sought after.

If you seek, the Father will give and give in abundance; the Father only loves, and in His love will give all that is needed to strengthen mankind to overcome the evil that exists.

Now the Father offers so much to His children, so much in love. Now the Father works many wonders through His chosen to show mankind, God is real and God is love. Now the Father looks on His children and showers them with gifts.

Now, why now? It is obvious, it is so clear. This time is an age of great sin, great apostasy, great heretics. This time is a time where God is hardly thought of. This time is a time of mankind's pride leading him into the arms of Satan.

How long does mankind think this time will last? If mankind goes hand in hand with Satan, does he not know Satan will demand his payment? It is a payment none will want to give; it is a payment all will try to avoid, but will be unable to do so, unless they are in God's love. There are two doors before mankind, walk through one and find eternal suffering, walk through the other and find eternal joy. Who would want the first?

There is a story of a man who was so far away from God that he did not know that God existed. He believed only in what he himself could do and what mankind's scientists could do. He believed that one day mankind would unlock the secret to death and be immortal. This man got older and older but mankind had still not overcome death; in desperation this man looked to herbs, to remedies, to mystical powers, but still he got older. His health began to fail and he could not accept he was going to die. The more he thought about death the more he wanted to live.

He heard one day of a guaranteed way to eternal life and so he went to seek it out. In a little while he came to a place called the fountain of youth. He asked if he could bathe in it but the owner said there was a price to pay. The man thought, whatever it is I will pay for it, for I can live forever, and so he inquired what it was.

"It is your soul," said the owner. "What's that?" thought the man, "It's nothing but an imaginary object," and so he gave it willingly. After he bathed in the fountain, he became young again and he was happy. The owner said, "Remember, your soul is mine." He couldn't care less! What's a soul? He went off singing and happy. On his way home he was crossing the road when a car came and knocked him down and killed him.

In death, he saw Jesus before him and then understood Jesus was real. He said to Jesus, "I didn't believe in You before, but now I know You are real. Please take me to heaven so I can be happy." Jesus said to him, "You do not belong to Me for you gave yourself freely to the devil, so that you could live forever. You have been told it is only God who gives life and that Satan only destroys life. When you made your agreement it was with the destroyer and he cannot keep his side of it, but you must keep yours." Satan took his soul and kept it in hell for eternity.

Today, mankind is making his own free choice. Which choices is he making? The choices which are influenced by deception or the choices influenced by love? The right choice will lead to Jesus, the other to hell.

†††

Lord Jesus—8/27/95

Today's generation has to come to terms with the reality of existence, it needs to wipe away the grime that covers its vision and see what life really is. For too long now mankind has blindly walked the path of life, not looking to see what life is, just taking for granted what he sees and feels is real. Anything that is outside mankind's understanding is often ignored or not believed. It is only what is tangible, what is seen as possible, because it fits in with the theories that mankind has developed, that is believed to be real. Everything else is discarded. What a dangerous thing to do, discard what you do not or cannot understand; what pride mankind has to do this.

The realities that mankind accepts may not be the true realities, may not be the truth. How can mankind know that they are? For mankind only sees them from his own perspective, from his own pride, from his own demands, from his own needs. What tainted vision! The life that mankind sees and believes to be the true life is only a moment in eternal life, yet so much importance is put on it. A moment that is there for the spirits of mankind to develop for their eternal life to come. A moment that is given so that God's family can develop in love to become love in Heaven.

Yet the explanation of life, which is the true explanation, is often rejected, mocked, abused, scorned. Why is the truth so difficult for mankind to accept, and lies or deceit so easy to accept? It is because mankind has placed his pride in front of his heart and soul and so blocks the truth of love being accepted and welcomed.

Lord Jesus—8/31/95

Under the veil of reason, all now can be explained away; all the mysteries of God and creation in the name of reason and science can be explained. This is what most of mankind believe and accept as the truth. Mankind no longer looks in faith but instead looks in disbelief or in excuses and reasons for hiding the truth. If something does not fit into mankind's understanding then it must be wrong, it must be imagination, it must not be true. If something does not agree with the way mankind expects or wants things to be, then it must be a mistake. Whatever exists, whatever is true, whatever is, can only be if mankind agrees that it is so.

What a strange way to be, what a strange way to live, to believe himself right in all things, himself having the understanding and answers to all things. What pride and what arrogance this shows in mankind, the same pride and arrogance that has been there from the beginning of mankind's walk away from God.

How insecure mankind must really be, for it is with insecurity that these thoughts and beliefs flourish. Insecurity makes a barrier to protect itself, a barrier that says anything that threatens my comfort, my beliefs, my feelings, is to be blocked out. Anything that challenges me is to be proven inferior or wrong. Anything that may open my inner self and put it at risk of being challenged is to be scoffed at.

Anything that may place me in a position of personal contact with a being who is superior to me, even if he only wants to love me, is to be avoided. All this shows how insecure and weak mankind really is. Each person knows when he looks within that he has these thoughts and feelings to a greater or lesser extent. Each person, even the strongest, knows those moments where he feels alone or lost. Each person has those moments of despair where he wonders what life is all about.

These are the hidden insecurities most try to deny or ignore. These are the feelings all have at some time in their life but refuse to admit to them. These are the feelings most respond to with anger, with pride, with arrogance. These are the feelings that mankind should explore and come to understand why they are there. These are the feelings that say mankind has turned from God and needs to come back to Him.

It is God who will help mankind defeat and overcome these insecurities, these fears. For it is in God that all the answers are to be found, and it is in God that the strength to overcome will be found. It is in God that pride and arrogance will disappear to be replaced with humility and love, which will bring all the graces that mankind needs to find his true self.

There is within each soul a special gift from God that will help each person overcome his pride, defeat his insecurities, and find the truth of life. The truth that is there for mankind to follow, the truth that is there to show mankind how to live, the truth that is God's love, the truth that is Jesus.

Each person only needs to open his heart and let this truth, this love fill him, for once he is filled with God's love, the strength, the power, the humility that envelops him will defeat all that is evil, all that is of the dark, all that is of sin. Mankind has within itself the most special gift of love that is from God, and is there only to help, guide, and protect.

God, when He created mankind, created a being filled with love. Mankind only needs to set this love free and rejoice in the glory of God's love. God offers to all this wonderful gift. It only needs to be accepted, welcomed, and embraced for each person to find his true self.

How many times since the beginning of creation has God told mankind He loves him? How many times has God offered His forgiveness and mercy? How many times has mankind refused? With his refusals mankind has slipped deeper and deeper into despair, into sin, into the dark.

In futility mankind looks for answers to his mistakes but never finds them, or when he does, he does not accept them because it makes mankind realize how wrong he has been. All the answers are there, all questions can be answered. Mankind just needs to accept the answers, accept the truth. Mankind must allow the truth to flourish and not deny it. People must bring the truth into their lives and live by it, for what is life if you do not live by what is true. A life ruled by lies, deceit, evil, is no life at all.

What if in your life you met someone who lied to you all the time, and every time you did what he suggested it ended in disaster. You would avoid this person, you would not listen to him and you certainly would not act on his suggestions. Mankind today does listen, does act, and does not avoid this situation... he actually welcomes it, welcomes evil.

It is so obvious, but mankind listens over and over, acts over and over and then ends in disaster. Famines, wars, pestilence, diseases, disaster after disaster are welcomed and embraced and then he wonders why they happen.

If a man kept beating you, kept hurting you, kept abusing you, kept killing your family, surely you would turn away. Today the evil one does these things but hides them in half truths and lies. Brush away this layer of deceit and realize what is happening to mankind and then turn away from it, turn into the ever loving arms of Jesus.

Lord Jesus—9/10/95

The Heart of Jesus is there waiting to help, the Heart of Jesus is opened wide and waiting to embrace all in love, and the Heart of Jesus is there longing for the love of His children. Hide yourselves in the Heart of Jesus and find the true life that awaits all.

155.

Hide yourselves in the Heart of Jesus and find Heaven. It is when you place yourself completely into Jesus' Heart and allow whatever Jesus wants to happen in your life, that you will find the truth of God's love. Your life will then become one with Jesus, your every breath will become a breath for Jesus, your every moment will become a moment for Jesus, every heart-beat will be a beat of love for Jesus.

When you do this, nothing can harm you, nothing can destroy you, nothing can take you from God. Then every look you give will be a look of love, every word you speak will be a word of love, and every thought you have will be a thought of love.

This is what you were created to be, this is how you are supposed to live, this is the true self that most deny or keep hidden but can release in an explosion of love, when placed in the Heart of Jesus.

Imagine life with everyone wanting to help, wanting to love, wanting to share. Imagine that and then see that it can happen, it can become the truth, it can become life on earth.

It needs each person to start to live this way, it needs each person to take up the challenge and not wait for others to do it first. As each individual does so, it will spread like a small ripple in a pond at first, and grow and grow until it becomes a tidal wave of love that floods the earth and brings peace and joy to mankind once more.

It needs each person to say, today I will start to change; I will place myself in Jesus' Heart and let Jesus guide my every step in life. Today I will start to love; today I commit myself to the battle of good over evil. Today I join the army of God's love and become a sign of love in the world.

There will be difficult times, times when you feel angry, times when you feel hurt, times when you doubt. In these moments see the Heart of Jesus before you and enter it, then see how Jesus acted and would react to moments like these and find the strength to overcome in Jesus' love. It is when you do this you show you truly are God's child, you show you truly are God's chosen, you show you truly belong to Jesus. This is how the ripple becomes a tidal wave, this is how the Word of God reaches all people, this is how evil is defeated, not with anger, not with hate, not with violence, but with love...always love.

Chapter 2.

The Sacraments—
Messages from God, The Son

Lord Jesus—9/24/95

After so long a time since mankind was created and then first sinned, there is little difference in the hearts of mankind. They are still simple, pure hearts that are created from love to exist in love. In that simplicity mankind has been easily confused and has become an easy victim of evil. A pure spirit tainted by the dark, by evil, is no longer pure; that spirit starts to decay into a pit of evil, a receptor of sin, an infectious spirit which affects those who come in contact with it. So, what was once pure becomes the opposite of what it was created to be. A pure spirit lost is such a sadness to God; a pure spirit taken to the evil one is such a tragedy for all.

To prevent this from happening, the Father in His mercy gave Himself through Me, His Son Jesus on the cross, as a sacrifice to defeat evil. I, through My sacrifice gave those people who were being infected by sin, were being taken by evil, another chance to cleanse themselves through My Sacred Blood. This cleansing is offered to all mankind's spirits through the Sacraments I gave to My children.

The Sacraments are the gifts God is offering to all so that they may cleanse their very souls and fill them with God's Love and God's Mercy. The Sacraments are so very special for it is through them that spiritual union with God and spiritual strength are found. The Sacraments offer all of mankind the answers they have been searching for, for so long.

The Sacraments bring each person into physical and spiritual contact with their Creator through Me, His Son Jesus, and through His Holy Spirit. If each person were to look with eyes of faith and belief to the Sacraments each one would find the peace, the love, the forgiveness, and the joy that each needs.

So many now are lost and confused, searching for that elusive peace of mind, comfort of soul and tranquillity of love that they never seem to find. It is there for them in the Sacraments; this is what the Sacraments are for, to bring God's peace, comfort, and tranquillity. Once a person truly opens himself and allows the grace of each Sacrament to fill him, then he will never search again.

Once the overwhelming love of God engulfs a person, he never wants to leave. The Sacraments are so much more than mankind believes, and this is why they are so important for each person to receive. With every gift of a Sacrament, the soul is strengthened, the person brought deeper into God's love. This is why evil tries to stop mankind receiving these special graces. Evil makes the Sacraments seem unimportant, inconsequential, unnecessary. Evil makes little of what is so great. Evil makes fun of what is so important and evil makes lies out of what is truth.

JESUS

Now understand why God gave the Sacraments and when you understand, return to them. God asked that each one be baptized in His name, the name of Jesus. This is to say the person is God's, this person is to spend eternity in God's love. This Sacrament is to claim what God created as His own, His child.

This Sacrament places a barrier between evil and this child of God. This sacrament is saying, I give this child to God who in His mercy gave him to me. This Sacrament is a reaffirming of the bond between parents and their Father in Heaven. This Sacrament is a strengthening of God's love within this family. This Sacrament is the first moment of a life commitment to God.

As a child grows it is influenced by those around it; it is attacked over and over by evil, for evil knows the value of one person to God. There is a constant battle of good versus evil; while the child is young he cannot defend himself, so God in His mercy gives each an angel to watch over and protect him. The battle rages around the child with the angel standing firm in God's love to defend this young one.

As the child starts to develop, it then becomes part of the fight, a little at a time it enters into the battle and the angel slowly withdraws. This is so the person can develop his own strength in God's love, a strength to see this being the doorway to Heaven. Mistakes will be made, sins will be committed as this is part of the growing of the child. As the sins accumulate on the soul it strives to be cleansed, to have this weight lifted from it. God in His mercy gives the Sacrament of Confession; that is what this Sacrament is for, to lift this burden from the soul and to allow it to develop more and more in God's love.

The Holy Spirit fills the soul of the one in sin and lifts all the pain, all the confusion and shows the person God's loving mercy. This happens when the person confesses truly and tries not to sin again. If a person confesses but intends to carry on sinning, then it is not a true confession and the stain of sin remains and often grows. So the Sacrament of Confession is there to cleanse, to fill with the Holy Spirit and bring closer to God. Confession also strengthens a person for the battle ahead which does not end until the next life is attained. Confession is a gift to heal, to strengthen, to purify, and to bring closer to God.

A person exists by spiritual food not by physical food and so God in His mercy supplies the food of life for all people in Holy Communion. When the Holy Bread and Wine are received in the Sacrament of the Eucharist, this person is granted the most special of all graces, that of being one with God, of being in union with the Lord.

When the person opens himself completely to God and lets the pure love of God fill his entire being, the strength of God lifts this being to a higher level, lifts this being to God's glory, lifts this person on high for the next battle. To have one's very being filled with God is so special that the evil one will try even harder to destroy this soul.

The answer is to receive the Lord more and more and in this way be so strong in God's love that evil cannot harm you. Communion with God is a unique gift to mankind, a gift that is there to feed man's very soul.

So with the Sacraments the being grows and is strengthened and, as the person grows in body and in soul, a choice is given. A choice to confirm your belief in God, a choice to invite the Holy Spirit to fill your spirit with His Light and Love. With this sacrament the very soul comes alive in God, the spirit shines in God's glorious gift of His Holy Spirit. At this time a true follower of God who has lived his or her life for God's glory, is given a protector to help this person that is trying to walk the path to God. The Saint who is chosen is there to help fight the battle with evil, is there to guide, to love, to watch over, and finally welcome into Heaven. A special gift to a Saint and a special grace for mankind.

Now the person is fully prepared for what lies ahead, prepared to stand against evil with the help of the Sacraments. Unfortunately, as many develop, the pressure of evil increases upon them and in their weakness they give in so easily. All of a sudden the Sacraments which are there to help them no longer seem valid, no longer seem worthwhile, no longer seem to be needed. This shows that evil is overcoming this being and as this person is no longer receiving the gifts of God, he does not have the strength to fight the evil one.

In the confusion the person searches for peace and comfort elsewhere, he looks for so much but finds so little. The evil one keeps attacking, distracting this person from the true graces he should be seeking and receiving. He wanders through life on earth lost and confused; with this confusion the person goes further and further away from God. When he comes in contact with those closer to God, he feels uncomfortable, uneasy and in response becomes angry and filled with hate.

Now he is sinking deeper and deeper into the dark, growing further and further away from God's love. It is these times that the Sacraments are so important for it is through them that the person can be brought back to God's love. The forgiveness, the mercy, the union with God can bring a child of God that is almost destroyed back to life in God.

How do you get these persons to return to the Sacraments as sometimes they are so lost they will not listen?

It is through the Sacraments and prayer that they can be saved. If one who loves them offers them the Sacraments, they receive for others as well as themselves, then God will allow the Sacrament to be shared. Little by little the lost ones will start to feel the benefit of God's gracious love and in time they will be strong enough to stand against evil and to return to the Sacraments themselves. It often takes many years on earth but know that this is just a moment in Eternity.

It may seem that there is no change but in most there will be, but it will be a spiritual change. For some it may be towards the end of their lives on earth before they return to God's love, but as long as they return, this is the important thing. Never give up, persevere in your offering of the Sacraments for those you love and then in Eternity see the rewards of your battle.

Those who do not return to God's love will then have been given every opportunity to change and return. They will have had Angels, Saints and those who love them fighting for them, standing against evil for them, offering them the helping hand of love. So much done for them and still some will refuse; then they make their own free choice to welcome eternal pain and suffering; they will have refused by their own free will God's love and so they must be given what they seek.

God offers mankind love in His Sacraments and God offers free choice in His love.

As you can see, the Sacraments are here to help, to strengthen, to fill with love, to forgive. The Sacraments are here to help in the battle against evil and to strengthen in the fight against sin. The Sacraments are here to forgive your weaknesses and to fill you with love to overcome your temptations.

The Sacraments of God are for mankind to grow in and for evil to be defeated.

The Sacraments of God are for mankind to learn through and develop in.

The Sacraments of God are for mankind from God's Heart.

Chapter 3.

The Church—
Messages from God, The Son

Lord Jesus—9/30/95

My Church came into being the day I gave My life for My children on earth: the new Church of God that was to bring all My children back to My love: the new Church of God that was to show the way to Heaven in humility and love.

In the beginning it was small with a few followers but then, as My apostles and My disciples spread my love throughout mankind, the Church grew and grew. So many sought My love, so many wanted to be saved, and so many began to follow My Word.

When I gave my dear friend and Apostle Peter the keys to Heaven, I did it so all would know that My Word, My Spirit would be spoken through this man. Peter led the early church deeper into My Heart by his love of Me and his example of how to live for God in humility and trust. When I chose another to spread My word to the gentiles, Peter did not complain, Peter did not feel hurt or rejected, Peter accepted in humility My love. Peter accepted in love My decision for he knew this was part of My plan for the saving grace to be offered to all mankind.

Peter welcomed Paul into My Church and encouraged him to continue to spread my Word and My Gifts to all who sought them. Peter saw that if I wanted My Holy Spirit to come into others then it must be, for it is God's wish. Peter, who guided in love the foundation of the early Church, sought to bring My love to all but to bring it by My wishes, not his. Peter who opened his arms in love to all mankind, wanting only to show My Love and Mercy to everyone.

When Peter gave the keys of Heaven to the next head of My Church, he gave him the same power I gave Peter, for when the keys were passed on, I passed on My Blessing. The responsibility that came with leading My Church was the responsibility of spreading My Word and My Love to all, to welcome all into My Church, to welcome all in humility and love.

To be a living example of the love of God, and to be a loving example of the life that leads to God. This example was to show all mankind the true faith in God, the faith that comes with being filled with the Holy Spirit and trusting completely in God. Sometimes human emotions, human needs and human desires would get in the way, but with trust in the Holy Spirit these would be overcome.

As time went on and the Church grew more and more, and then as political and even military pressures were put upon the Church, sometimes the trust in God that was supposed to be there was forgotten. This was not because of God turning His back on the Church but it was due to the humanness of those within the Church. Sometimes fear, greed, lust, power and wealth influenced decisions that should have only been influenced by the Holy Spirit. With trust in God, complete trust in God, the mistakes made would have been avoided. In His love, the Holy Spirit took the wrong choices made within the Church and turned them into victories for God, turned them into a strengthening of the Church.

Each time there was a weakness or an error appearing in the Church, the evil one, of course, would do his best to exploit it and try to destroy God's Church by creating division and unrest. Within the Church many good people were, and still are, confused by the evil one, confused into disagreeing with what God's chosen leader asks, confused even to disagree with the commandments of God. When God said "Thou shalt not kill," there is no justification for changing it, and when the Holy Father says abortion is wrong, he is only restating God's commandment and there is no justification for opposing it.

The evil one, however, makes some within the Church disagree, and then fester in their discontent. Often what happens is they leave the Church, even form churches of their own. This is how Satan tries to divide the Church so that he can conquer it. The new churches are then formed on what man disagrees with from God and in their pride many do not, cannot, and will not admit to this.

If a church is formed from man's pride and not his humility, from what man wants and not what God wants, from what man sees as right not from what God says is right, then it can only be deception to take good people from God. If, when there are mistakes made within the Church of God, those who see them pray for God's will to be done and accept God's will in humility, then the mistakes will be overcome. If they do not do this, then it is their pride, their humanity that is ruling their heart, and not the love of God. Remember how Peter acted in humility and love and imitated his actions for God.

Remember also there is only one God and there should be only one Church, the Church that came from God's Son Jesus through Peter and then his successors.

The Church that is universal, the Church that is for all, the Church of God that is His Body, one Body. The divisions are not of God, they are of mankind. Become united in one Church, the true Church that follows Jesus' Word, accepts Jesus' truth and worships the Holy Trinity as the one true God.

Chapter 4.

The Advice—
Messages from God, The Holy Trinity
and from Our Lady

God, The Father—2/3/95

As Veronica wiped the blood and sweat from My Son's face, she showed that man really did love God. With her act of love and compassion she showed that the love had not died. With her comforting of My Son with this one act she touched His spirit deeply, she strengthened Him in His moment of need. Veronica's name echoed throughout time and throughout Heaven when she loved her Lord publicly and openly without fear. This act lifted Veronica to glory in Heaven and this is how it will be for all those who will love the Lord Jesus My Son openly without fear.

God, The Father—2/3/95

As My Son Jesus carried the cross upon His shoulder, I wept tears of joy and tears of sorrow...the joy that man's sins would be forgiven and that they would be welcomed in Heaven if they followed My Son's way...the sorrow to see my sweet Son suffer so, to see Him treated as if He were a sinner; but how else to forgive sins except to take the pain for them.

God, The Father—2/3/95

A step forward can be a step backward, and a step backward can be a step forward. If you step forward without prudence, it can take you backward, and if you step backward in love, it can be a step forward.

God, The Father—2/4/95

Temptation means nothing when you think of Jesus. Thoughts of the dark disappear when you think of Jesus. Joy returns when you think of Jesus. Just think of Jesus.

God, The Father—2/4/95

An offering was made in the temple and an offering was made on the Cross. The life of My Son Jesus was a complete offering, a complete giving, a complete sacrifice. My Son Jesus' life was the ultimate offering...an offering of love.

God, The Father—2/4/95

Simon carried the Cross on his back with My Son Jesus. Simon showed that all men need to share this burden with Jesus so that they can lift the pain from men. The pain of self and sin.

God, The Father—2/5/95

Sweat of Love, Drops of Blood, Sweat of Forgiveness, Drops of Blood, Sweat of Mercy, Drops of Blood. Find the Love, Forgiveness and Mercy through My Son Jesus who shed His Blood for mankind.

Lord Jesus—2/5/95

Through My time on the cross My pain and suffering increased as I thought about all the sins man has and will commit. I saw each sin and I felt that pain each caused; I saw each sin and felt the torment each created. I watched, I felt, I became full of all the sins' effects on mankind's souls and then with the giving of My Blood to the Father I cast all of this into the abyss from whence it came.

I opened My Heart and let My Love flow out and wash away all the darkness created by sin. I opened My Spirit and filled the whole of creation with God's forgiveness. I opened My Body and let mankind be free of all the misery he has created or accepted. I shower mankind with My Gifts, My Graces, My Love, Myself.

What more can I give, what more can I do, what more does mankind need to change? Whatever it is, it is in Me; whatever it is, I have it; whatever it is, ask for it and I will give it, for I love mankind and always will.

The Holy Spirit—2/6/95

The fire of love burns within, even if at times you cannot feel it, it is still there. The fire of love fills you as you need it, it fills you with My gifts to do My work for the Father and sweet Lord Jesus. The fire of love is with you always, just know this and be happy.

The Holy Spirit—2/6/95

A flower opens to show its glory, a tree bears fruit to feed its friends, a person shares love to fill others with joy. All of creation is here to help; all of creation is here to share, and all of creation shows God's Mercy.

The Holy Spirit—2/6/95

Fruit of Love, Flower of Joy, Friend of All, Jesus.
Sweet of Sweets, Joy of Joys, Love of Loves, Jesus.
Tower of Strength, Table of Love, Truth of God, Jesus.

God, The Father—2/7/95

In love with the whole of mankind,
In love with all of creation,
In love with all of Me is the Way to true
happiness, the happiness of God.

God, The Father—2/7/95

Light of God, Love of God.
Light for man, Light from God.
Love for man, Love from God.
Jesus, My Son.
Passion of love in man,
Passion of love in God,
Passion of love in eternity,
Jesus, My Son.
Fathomless Heart,
Endless Mercy,
Eternal Love,
Jesus, My Son.
Blood of Joy,
Body of Love,
Soul of the Savior in Jesus, My Son.
Font of Forgiveness,
Pool of Precious Blood,
Bread of Beauty in Jesus, My Son.
Eyes of Compassion,
Heart of Love,
Spirit of Forgiveness in Jesus, My Son.

The Holy Spirit—2/8/95

Flame of God, Fire of Faith,
Dove of Peace, Calming Waters, Wind of Mercy.
The Holy Spirit, God's Spirit, Jesus' Spirit, one
and the same.

The Holy Spirit—2/8/95

Place yourself in Jesus' Heart, never to leave, never
to part. Lie in peace in Jesus' arms, never to hurt
nor fear any harm.
Sleep in comfort in Jesus' hands, never to fret and
never to give in to man's demands.

*Vision—2/9/95—Vision in church of the Father with
the Eucharist in His left hand saying, "This is My Son."*

God, The Father—2/10/95

Father of Fathers,
Love of Loves,
Light of Lights,
Your Father in Heaven.

God, The Father—2/10/95

Under a flag of love you must stand, and you
must stand firm in love.
Under a flag of love you must speak, and you must
speak of love.
Under a flag of love you must shine, and you must
shine with love, the love that is My Son Jesus.

God, The Father—2/11/95

Beside My Son's suffering is the suffering of man,
for it is man's suffering that caused the suffering of
My Son. Jesus wants to show man that man's pain

can be defeated by trusting in Him, trusting in Me, His Father, and trusting in the Holy Spirit. Jesus showed that He trusted completely, and with this trust He overcame sin and death. Mankind can overcome these as well, if he will only trust in Me, My Son, and My Spirit. Just trust.

God, The Father—2/11/95

To show love of Jesus, many become brides of Christ, many become brothers of Jesus, and many become servants of Christ. Those religious who devote themselves to God's love need to understand that when they declare themselves for Christ, it should be a complete giving. Worldly possessions should not be a concern, only spiritual, for when you are Jesus' He will provide.

How many priests and nuns worry about the clothes they wear, the cars they drive, the possessions they have? How many religious do not wear the gowns that show they are the Lord's? By wearing the dress of the religious they show the world they are God's, but by wearing dress of the world they show their vanity.

ttt

Lord Jesus—2/11/95

Son of God, Son of Man.
Son of Love, Son of Purity.
Son of Light, Son of Immaculate Conception.
When times are without love, without hope and without mercy, turn to Me and find your Love, Hope, and Mercy in My Divine Heart.
Put your trust in Me as did all those in Heaven.
Put yourself in Me as did all the Saints.
Put yourself in My hands as did all the martyrs.
Then become one with Me forever.
Long ago came a man, a man of faith.
Long ago came God.
Long ago came God as man and soon He comes again. *(Jer. Chap. 10:14 & Chap. 11:12)*

Vision—2/11/95—Vision of Jesus walking on the water. He said, "As the water firmed at My touch so will mankind's hearts."

God, The Father—2/12/95

Cross of Jesus, cross of Man.
Cross of Pain, cross of Sorrow.
Cross of Forgiveness, Cross of Redemption.
Cross of Love.

God, The Father—2/12/95

Jesus Christ, True God, True Man.
A Divine Mystery, a Divine Revelation, a Divine Love.

God, The Father—2/12/95

In love with His children, He gave His all.
In love with His brothers and sisters, He gave His all.
In love with His Father, He gave His all.
He gave His love to all for God.

The Holy Spirit—2/12/95

Trust in God is the strongest weapon against the dark.
With your trust you show your love of God and with your love you defeat evil.

The Holy Spirit—2/12/95

Grace of God, Forgiveness.
Gift of God, Love.
Generosity of God, Mercy.
God who forgives and loves all in His Mercy.

God, The Father—2/13/95

Upon a hill stood the cross of Redemption, upon a hill stood the Cross of Forgiveness, and upon a hill stood the Cross of Love. Now mankind needs to stand under its shadow and feel the true strength of God. Now mankind needs to stand under its shadow and show its true strength. Now mankind needs to stand under its shadow and show its true love of God, for this is the only way home to Heaven.

God, The Father—2/13/95

Until the end of time I will love mankind, until the beginning of eternal life I will want to save mankind, and until mankind understands what this means, I will keep telling it why.

Vision—2/13/95—After communion, 9:45 a.m., I had a vision of God's light shining from the Tabernacle with the words Truth, Justice, Faith, Hope, Charity, Love and Compassion appearing. The Lord said that these are all within the Tabernacle. Then the light shone on my chest and formed a white cross and the Lord said, "The Cross of Love."

The Holy Spirit—2/13/95

Under the pain of death, My Son Jesus, forgave man.
Under the suffering of His Soul, My Son Jesus, redeemed man, and,
Under the torment of His Spirit, My Son Jesus, gave man the way to Heaven.
The Way that is Jesus Christ.

The Holy Spirit—2/13/95

Alone with God, alone with Love,
Alone with your Friend.

The Holy Spirit—2/13/95

Among those God chooses are the ones who try to live as Jesus did. Among those God chooses are the ones who run the race of love until the end. Among those God chooses are those who succeed in becoming eternal love as the Saints in Heaven. Now God chooses again. Will those children be strong enough? They will be, if they only trust in My Son Jesus' love.

God, The Father—2/14/95

Under the cross stands the Mother of Jesus and the Mother of man, full of sorrow for mankind, full of pity for the poor, full of sadness for sinners. Lift her heart with the love you send her in your prayers, and lift her heart when you call her Mother.

Lord Jesus—2/14/95

My mother loves you as she loves all mankind. My mother watches over you as she watches over all mankind, and My mother cares for you as she cares for all mankind.

My mother calls you son, as she wants to call all men. My mother calls you family, as she wants to call all mankind, and My mother calls you true child of God, as she wants all mankind to be.

My mother loves you and watches and cares for you. My mother calls you son, part of her Heavenly family and son of God's Mercy. My mother is your mother and My mother just loves you.

God, The Father—2/15/95

A way to find God's love is the way of prayer;
A way to find God's forgiveness is the way of Jesus;
A way to find God is praying to Jesus, for He is God.

Lord Jesus—2/15/95

Mother took My hand and walked with Me through the markets in Jerusalem, and as we walked she showed Me My lost children arguing and fighting among themselves. Together we looked on in sorrow, as all that seemed to matter was worldly goods. The Father of all was ignored, His House overflowing with merchants more interested in profit and bargains, more interested in self and sin. The soul of man was ignored as if it did not exist; the Father took second place to man and money.

Mother's heart was so heavy to see all these lost ones, all these who needed to be guided back to God. When mother looked into My eyes, she looked with her heart and she knew I was here for this. When Mother saw the Savior before her, she knew it would be a painful path...a path of rejection, a path of sorrow, but also a path of joy. When mother saw her small Son before her and saw what He had to overcome, she despaired and worried for her Son, but she trusted in God and knew all would be well.

As she held My hand tighter and let her love flow into My spirit, I returned this love with the comfort and joy of God touching her soul. She knew I would be strong enough to take mankind's hand and lead it back home to the loving Father in Heaven. With this knowledge deep in her heart, mother could face all the trials and tribulations ahead, for she knew the love of God.

Lord Jesus—2/15/95

Over and over I tell mankind of My love because I want mankind to listen; I will keep telling mankind until it does. It is the same with man's children. Does he not keep telling and explaining to them how to live? How else would they learn except from their parents? So it is with God; I will keep guiding, loving, explaining, until everyone listens and grows to be the spirits The Father created them to be.

✝✝✝

Lord Jesus—2/15/95

As drops of rain fall on the ground, so fall My tears; as drops of rain settle on the earth, so settles My blood, and as drops of rain become a stream, so become My tears and blood, as a torrent to wash man's sins away.

Mankind now must start to sail in this stream of love or he risks being washed away. Mankind now should wash himself in this stream to become one with Me, and mankind must join Me as a torrent of love and beauty to wash away the evil from this planet. Show your love by living in this stream, show your trust by walking in this stream, and show your humility when you lead others to this stream.

God, The Father—2/16/95

True to God, true to love, true to truth is the way to Heaven.

True to self, true to others, true to all is the way to God.

True to the Word, true to the Way, true to My Son Jesus, is the way to God, for He is God with Me and My Holy Spirit, forever and ever, Amen.

Vision—2/16/95—When praying in front of Mother's statue, Our Lady came to me, put her arm around me and said, "Hush, rest quietly in my love." I tried to, but the evil one appeared; then Mother held me close and said, "Let my love protect you." The evil one disappeared and I felt at peace.

Lord Jesus—2/17/95

Prayers of the people are always welcome in My heart, so ask them to pray often.

177.

Lord Jesus—2/17/95

Under a cloud that hides sin, stand most of My children,
Under a cloud that deceives them into believing right is wrong, and wrong is right.
Under a cloud that covers My love for them.

Lord Jesus—2/17/95

Fruit that falls on the ground and is eaten is the sweetest fruit. It brings joy to those who consume it. This is how My love is, waiting to be eaten, waiting to bring joy to those who consume it.

God, The Father—2/18/95

Falling into My hands are the souls of mankind; many though, slip through My fingers because they wish to. Oh how I want them to know what they bring themselves; Oh how I want them to know what they lose. Tell them, show them, and save them in My Son Jesus' Name.

God, The Father—2/19/95

Seeing the world in such pain and sorrow fills Me with sadness. How I want My children to change so they can be with Me but they turn their backs on Me. They treat Me with contempt. Why do they do this when all I offer is goodness? It is because they have been blinded by evil which looks good. It is because they have been seduced by evil which tastes sweet but is really bitterness.

Oh! How My heart breaks. Oh! How My heart grieves. Oh! How I sorrow. How many parents feel this way through their children's lives, but then see them change for the better as wisdom comes to them? So it will be with mankind when it will change. But how many will be lost before it does?

Our Lady—2/19/95 (after seeing ouija board on movie)

Corruption of minds, corruption of spirits, corruption of souls. It is everywhere in the programs you watch. It is now normal to show things of evil just as a bit of fun, as a child's game.

That is how evil is everywhere attacking the young and weak, the innocent. It then turns them into unwitting servants, unwitting accomplices, and unwilling givers of themselves to Satan.

Our Lady—2/19/95

The perseverance that comes with loving is the strength that comes from God. The strength that comes from God perseveres forever in love.

Our Lady—2/19/95

To be a servant of God is to be a servant of all, and to be a servant of all, is to be a servant of God.

Our Lady—2/19/95

Service in love, is service for God.
Service in love, is service for God's glory, and
Service in love, is service in God's mercy.

Our Lady—2/19/95

A mother's love is here for all,
A mother's help is here for all, and
A mother is here for all, if only they want her.

Our Lady—2/19/95

Son of God, Son of Mary.
Son of God, Son of Man, Son of David.

God, The Father—2/20/95

Alone inside, alone within, alone in love are those who deny Jesus.

Complete inside, complete within, complete in love are those who accept Jesus.

At one inside, at one within, at one in love are those who accept God's Son Jesus as Lord.

Lord Jesus—2/20/95

Sleep of sleeps is the sleep you have when you rest in Me.

Love of loves is the love you have when you live in Me.

Light of lights is the life you have when you shine for Me.

Lord Jesus—2/20/95

Praying the Rosary with your heart is such a special gift, that I treasure so much. It is the gift of your love, wrapped in flowers, with the sweetest perfume, that brings me so much pleasure. It is the gift of your love that you send to Me through My Mother and to My Father.

God, The Father—2/21/95

Babe of Bethlehem, Man of Mercy, Gift of God.

Savior of souls, Redeemer of rogues, Forgiver of the fallen.

Path of paths, Way of ways, Love of loves.

Jesus the Lord.

Lord Jesus—2/22/95

Friends of God sometimes become obstacles to God's work and God's love. How does this happen? How do those who love God end up opposing God without being aware of what they do? It is because of the sin that all are born from, the first sin of man. It is passed from generation to generation and it is this that makes it so easy for man to slip from God's way.

Lord Jesus—2/22/95

Sink into My Heart and fill yourself with My love,
Sink into My Soul and fill yourself with My mercy,
Sink into My Spirit and fill yourself with My gifts.
It is all there for you.
Just come to Me and ask for it.

Lord Jesus—2/23/95

Confusion of mind, confusion of soul, and confusion of spirit are all works of the evil one. Clear your mind, clear your soul, and clear your spirit in My Mercy.

Lord Jesus—2/23/95

My dear little ones, how I long to bring you to Me, how I long to hold you close to My heart and to let you be filled with My every grace. To come to Me, to be filled with Me you need to open yourself in prayer and in the sacraments; through these I can envelop you completely with My love. As you pray and as you receive My body and blood, be one with Me by thinking of My love for you.

God, The Father—2/24/95

Over time, mankind has become so lost he cannot find his way home. I sent My Son Jesus to show the way, but how many have listened? Now I want to show again how to come home to Me in Heaven; now I want to show again My Love. Will mankind listen this time?

Lord Jesus—2/24/95

Bread of Life, Food of Love,
Eternal Feast, the Eucharist.
Majestic Moments, Fruitful Filling,
Lasting Love, the Sacraments.
Celebration of Celebrations, Joy of Joys,
Hope of Hopes, the Mass.
Complete in the Mass, Complete in the Sacraments,
Complete in Prayer is My Love.
What a Mystery, what Love!

Lord Jesus—2/25/95

Love within a family can be difficult at times, but the strength of this love should overcome all. Love within a family can be the most wonderful love, if you hold on to it through all difficulties. Love within a family can strengthen the love of God, for God is love, and where there is love, there is God.

The Holy Spirit—2/26/95

Spirit of Love, Spirit of Joy, Spirit of God.
Spirit of Hope, Spirit of Strength, Spirit of God.
Spirit of Light, Spirit of Truth, Spirit of God.
The Holy Spirit, One with Jesus, One with the Father,
One in Truth, One in Eternity.

The Holy Spirit—2/26/95

Coming to the world is the One who saves all. Coming to the world is the One who loves all. Coming to the world is the One who joins all to the Father in Heaven. Jesus is the One and soon He comes.

Lord Jesus—2/26/95

Look to your friend for help, look to your friend for strength, look to your friend for comfort, your friend Jesus.

Lord Jesus—2/27/95

The love that is exposed to mankind through My sacrifice on the cross is a love mankind can never comprehend. It is so pure, so deep, so strong for it is God's love...a love that can overcome all, a love that can increase all in spirituality, a love that can strengthen all in hope, and a love that can open the doors to eternal life for all in Heaven

Lord Jesus—2/27/95

When clouds gather, look to the Son; when darkness surrounds, look to the Light; when all seems lost, look to the Way. The Son is the Light which shows the Way. The Way is the Son which is the Light. The Light is the Way which is the Son.

Lord Jesus—2/27/95

Trusting, trusting, trusting.
Giving, giving, giving.
Loving, loving, loving.
Trust, give and love.

God, The Father—2/28/95

Death of the spirit is the reward of evil, eternal life is the reward of Jesus. Eternal darkness comes with sin, life forever comes with love, the love that is Jesus.

Lord Jesus—2/28/95

Always remember the Blood I shed for you; I shed it because I love you; always remember the Mercy I gave you; I gave it because I love you and always remember the Forgiveness I washed your sins away with. I forgave you because I love you. I love all mankind, so this is there for them also if they truly seek it.

Lord Jesus—2/28/95

Hanging on the cross I showed My love; hanging on the cross I showed My mercy; hanging on the cross I showed My forgiveness. Now look upon it, see it for what it truly is, God loving man and God forgiving man. Shalom.

Vision—2/28/95—At church today vision of cross of red dripping blood, a white light shone behind it and the Father sat in front of it dressed in gold.

God, The Father—3/1/95

Come in humility, come in forgiveness, come in love.
Opposition demands humility, forgiveness, and love, for in this way you show your love of Me.
Turn sadness into joy, turn anger into love, turn hate into friendship through My love, Jesus.

Lord Jesus—3/1/95

Resting in Me is the most rewarding time; peace and tranquillity fill those who rest in Me. Trusting in Me is the most rewarding trust; strength and hope fill those who trust in Me. Love in Me is the most rewarding love; truth and joy fill those who love in Me. Rest, trust, and love in Me, and find true peace that strengthens you in hope and fills you with joy.

God, The Father—3/2/95

Father of Nations, Creator of All, Master of Races. This is your Father in Heaven.
Parent of Patience, Giver of Love, Receiver of Hopes. This is your Creator in Heaven.
Saving of Souls, Sharing of Love, Bringing of Joy. This is your God through His Son Jesus on earth.

Lord Jesus—3/2/95

My dear little ones, take a moment to look within; look and see your true selves. See yourselves for what you really are. See your faults, your weaknesses, your strengths, your innermost loves. See all this and then know I accept you as you are, I love you as you are and I want you with Me as you are. The Father created you as you are with the knowledge that sometimes you will fall, sometimes you will stumble, but this will not stop your God from loving you.

All I ask is that you love Me, that you love each other and that you try to live in My love by not sinning. If you try with a true heart, then I am waiting to lead you to an eternal life in Heaven. Now My children, look, see and accept yourselves as you are and be confident I love you as you are.

Our Lady—3/3/95

Underneath the surface lies the true self; when you peel away all the layers of self, you see what a person truly is. In most you find a lost soul struggling to survive in the dark. In some you find a soul sinking into the depths of hell, yet in others you find their souls lifting to Heaven in God's love. Those who are lost and those who are sinking can be saved by the light of God's mercy, if only they would come and stand in it.

Those who are lifted to Heaven must take other lost souls with them, by bringing God's light and love to them. They bring it by proclaiming Jesus as Lord, and by being an example of what it is to be a servant of Christ. The rewards for these are great indeed, the rewards of pleasing your God and being in His glory forever. A special place awaits those who serve the Lord, a seat at the table of Jesus.

Lord Jesus—3/3/95

In sickness and in health, accept My love.
In stress and in peace, accept My love.
In pain and in comfort, accept My love.
Accept it and become Mine.

Vision—3/4/95—At Mass after communion I had a vision of Jesus taking my hand and saying, "Come with Me." The Lord took me to a shining stream and said, "Drink from it," so I did. Jesus then said, "This is the Living Stream." The Lord then gave me a large cupful of the water and said, "Take this to My children to drink." As I took it, the river became red and Jesus said, "This is My Blood which is the Living Stream."

Lord Jesus—3/4/95

Drawing water from the stream soaks you in My love.

Sharing water from the stream fills others with My love.

Taking water to others, you become My love.

Lord Jesus—3/4/95

To the greedy, a lot seems a little,
To the needy, a little seems a lot.

God, The Father—3/4/95

Searching within you will find a deep recess, and when you look inside this, you will find your true self. Peel away all the outer layers, all superficial things and find what you truly are. When you see your true self, know that this is how I made you and this is how you should be, both outwardly and inwardly. When you achieve this, then you bring Me the greatest gift you can, yourself in love.

Vision—3/4/95—When praying the last decade of the glorious mystery, a vision of Our Lady with a golden crown of thorns. Later I was told it was the first Saturday in Lent and the first five are when Our Lady asked for prayer to lift the thorns from her. (Fatima Message)

The Holy Spirit—3/4/95

Lasting faith is found by love, and lasting love is found in faith.

Lasting truth is sought by love, and lasting love is sought in truth.

Lasting hope is the reward of love, and lasting love is the reward of hope.

†††

God, The Father—3/5/95

Son of Sons was, and is, Jesus,
Father of Fathers was, and is, Jesus,
Spirits of Spirits was, and is, Jesus.
Jesus is Lord and always will be
    together with the Father and the Spirit.
Three Loves, Three Lights, Three Truths,
    being One in the Trinity of Your Eternal God.

Lord Jesus—3/5/95

Daughters of the world need to become daughters of God, daughters of the world need to become sisters of Jesus, and daughters of the world need to become mothers of the new generation of God's children.

Lord Jesus—3/5/95

For those in need of God's forgiveness, a Sacrament can be given, but a Sacrament cannot be taken without forgiveness.

Lord Jesus—3/5/95—The Eucharist

Within this Bread is My Body and My Blood. This Bread truly is My Being, truly is My Love, truly is Me. Remember how I increased the loaves to feed those who came to listen to Me; remember how I fed them with an abundance remaining. The Eucharist is like this, no matter how often you receive Me, I have an abundance remaining to give you. The Eucharist, My Body, My Blood, Me, there for you, there for all, there to feed your souls, there to bring you to Me and Me to you, there to fill you with My Love, fill you with My Peace, Me. The Eucharist, My gift to mankind, My love to mankind, Myself to mankind. Receive the Eucharist and receive your Lord and receive His mercy.

†††

Lord Jesus—3/6/95

What a feast, what a joy, what a gift, all for you, all for mankind and all of Me in the Eucharist.

Lord Jesus—3/6/95

Fountain of Eternal Life, the Father.
Fountain of Eternal Love, the Son.
Fountain of Eternal Light, the Spirit.
One in Three and Three in One.
Mystery of Mysteries,
Question of Questions,
Wonder of Wonders,
The Trinity.

The Holy Spirit—3/6/95—(about gay mardi-gras)

Defilers of God's Temple, insulters of the Lord's love, destroyers of God's gift. This is what those do, who treat their bodies as theirs, to do with as they wish, regardless of why God gave it to them. With their abuse of God's gift they invite evil within and oh, how they will have to pay! Being blind to sin does not stop the payment that is demanded, does not stop the pain that Satan will bring, does not stop the destruction of your souls. Just change and ask for forgiveness and it is there for you.

The Holy Spirit—3/6/95

The cross of Jesus was weighed down by all mankind's sins. All the sins committed today weighed heavily upon His shoulders. Sweet Jesus never gave up even when He saw how low mankind would sink. He did not give up because He loves man regardless. He came to save all those who ask for help, for forgiveness, and for love. Sweet Lord Jesus asks only that you truly repent, that you see the error of your ways, and that you love His Father in Heaven. What a little to ask, but how the dark makes it look so

189.

much; what a lot Jesus has to give but oh, how the dark makes it seem so little! What a long path mankind has taken, the path of sin and suffering when he could have taken the short path of love and laughter that is Jesus Christ, the Redeemer, the Savior and the one true God with the Father and the Spirit. God's Son, God's Spirit, God, all one, all Love.

Lord Jesus—3/6/95

Just a walk along the path of true love is all it takes to bring you to Me.

Just opening your heart to My love is all it takes to bring you to the Father.

Just opening your spirit to My Spirit is all it takes to bring you to Heaven.

Lord Jesus—3/6/95

As I walked with My disciples along the shores of the Sea of Galilee, I brought them to understand who I truly was. I told them of My destiny on the cross, I told them of My resurrection in three days, and I told them this would show the glory of God's love.

When I told them of My death they were afraid, afraid to be left alone. They wanted Me with them always but they did not understand I was, I am and I will be, forever. Their fear of being left alone to fend for themselves, to walk the way of the Father alone, to face all opposition alone was their humanness.

Spiritually they knew I would be there, but their humanness blocked the acceptance of this, even though I, their God, spoke directly to them, performed many miracles in front of them, and touched their souls with My soul, they still could not understand God's ways.

Imagine then, how it was for those who saw all, heard all, were told all and still did not understand. Imagine then how hard it is for those who only know

Me through the Word of the Holy Scripture. Imagine how much harder it is for them to accept and believe. Do you not believe that, if I appeared today and performed all that I did in Galilee, the whole world would turn to Me for love and forgiveness? Surely with all those signs they would have to believe.

Mankind, however, is not like that; at first they would look in amazement, many would follow and proclaim Me as Lord but then many more would question and doubt. They would look for explanations, they would look to see how I was deceiving them, and then they would look away and say, "He comes to lead us from God, for if He was the Messiah He would not appear so. If He was the Messiah He would be surrounded by Angels, He would be lifted in glory by the Father, He would be a King amongst men.

"If He was the Messiah I would know because I understand Holy Scripture, I understand God's ways, I would know." Isn't this the pride that man has always had? This pride would stop many from accepting Me, acknowledging Me as God's Son, just as this pride stopped the Pharisees, the Sadducees, and the High Priests believing that I was God's true Son.

So you see, mankind is still doubting, disbelieving, and following its pride instead of following its humility. No wonder you struggle, for this is the way of man and you are a man. Now come to terms with this and know it is part of your very nature since Adam and Eve first sinned. Come to terms with it but do not accept it or allow it to lead you away from Me. Come to terms with it and know I am there, I am with you, you are Mine forever; it is only your inner pride that keeps you from understanding fully what awaits you. It is only your doubts which block My love flowing completely through you.

Look then to My Disciples, My Apostles and see that they were the same until they undertook My work as their way of showing their love for Me.

Lord Jesus—3/7/95

Love conquers all, love builds all, love strengthens all. Sin defeats the weak, sin destroys everything it touches, sin weakens the strong. The choice is obvious, choose love and win, choose love and live, choose love and become one with Me for I am love, I am Jesus.

Lord Jesus—3/8/95

Turn your pride from pride of self to pride of God, turn your love from love of self to love of God, and turn your humility into an expression of faith and service in God.

Lord Jesus—3/8/95

Until the world worships and loves God openly, it can never see Heaven on earth.

Lord Jesus—3/8/95

Whenever in doubt, turn to Me, whenever in trouble, turn to Me, whenever you want, turn to Me...for I am there waiting for your prayers.

Lord Jesus—3/8/95

Awaiting the time mankind shows his true self. Awaiting the day mankind lets his true self shine through. Awaiting the time mankind accepts his true self for what he is. His true self is God's creation, God's love, and God's children.

Lord Jesus—3/8/95

Family of man, family of God, family of love. Mankind is this, but most do not accept or understand, most do not believe or show openness to each other

or to God. What a terrible waste of a gift, the gift
of oneness in God with each other.

†††

God, The Father—3/8/95

Cross of Love, Cross of Jesus, Cross of God, for
Jesus is Love and is God.
Hope of Love, Hope of Jesus, Hope of God.
Man is that hope who through Jesus will find God.
Scent of Flowers, Scent of Love, Scent of God.
Jesus the Flower of Love that is God.

God, The Father—3/9/95

When a child is seen to struggle, his father helps.
If this is so with human fathers, then imagine how
I will help when My children struggle. If a father lifts
a burden from his child's shoulders, then imagine how
I will lift all burdens from My children. If a father
soothes a worried child, imagine then how I will
comfort My children in times of worries. I who have
all to comfort, help and lift burdens from, will do it
through My Son Jesus.

Our Lady—3/9/95

The nails pierced my heart as they entered my
Son's hands and feet. The pain filled me completely
as I shared in the lifting of man's sins to the Father
for forgiveness. I felt all the pain within Jesus as I
looked into my Son's eyes, eyes that were filled with
sadness and joy. Sadness at man's foolishness and joy
at the defeat of evil. As I watched the blood run down
my sweet Son's face, my tears ran red down my face
in union with Jesus' suffering. As He lifted His head
and cried out in agony to the Father for man's
forgiveness, I could not only see the glory He brought
to God, but I could feel the struggle within to
persevere with His giving to the end.

How my heart broke to be there unable to touch and comfort my Son in His time of need. As a mother I just wanted it to stop, I just wanted my Son's pain to end.

As his Father's servant I knew this must be and so I kept silent except for my prayers to God to ease the pain and to end it soon. As man's mother I now ask the Father the same, to end the pain and suffering in the world and to bring His children home to Him. My heart breaks again, my eyes cry tears of blood, and my prayers ask the Father to intervene and bring this time of pain to an end.

The Father listens and will answer my prayers and mankind will be saved. First, though, mankind needs to be shown what he has done to himself and then be shown the way to God's forgiveness. There is only one way and it was shown on the cross; the way is Jesus.

Our Lady—3/9/95

As a mother I look upon you, my children and want to embrace you, to hold you close to me and bring you to my Son, Jesus. I open my heart to you and invite you within and when you enter my love you will only find the way to Jesus. Like you, I am a servant of God, like you, I am completely human and, like you, I long to show my love to God.

Let us join together and express our love for God in prayer and in the Sacraments you receive. I am watching over you all at every moment, watching and waiting to celebrate together with you when you come to my Son, Jesus.

Vision—3/10/95—Vision of Our Lady with crown of roses; afterwards a smell of roses in O.L.V.

Lord Jesus—3/10/95

The joy of forgiveness is such a sweet joy. The happiness of being friends again is a wonderful happiness. The sweet words that say, I forgive you, ring deep in your heart and fill you with love. Understand that you must be forgiving of others as you expect them to forgive you, understand and accept. You will, as others will, make mistakes; understand and love.

Lord Jesus—3/10/95

My Blood becomes one with My Body when they are joined in the Eucharistic Bread. When you eat this Bread you take Me within and then you become one with Me. Your body and your blood become one with Mine and so you become the sign of Jesus to others. Everyone who receives the Eucharist receives Me and becomes one with Me, in Communion with Me. Everyone who receives Me becomes My sign to others. How many accept this and truly show they are one with Me?

Lord Jesus—3/10/95

Vision of Loveliness, Vision of Joy, Vision of Motherly Care. Mary, My Mother.
Vision of Peace, Vision of Comfort, Vision of Gentleness. Mary, My Mother. Vision of Grace, Vision of Majesty,
Vision of Quiet Love, Mary, My Mother.

Lord Jesus—3/10/95

Truth overcomes all. Love overcomes all. Faith overcomes all. I am Truth, I am Love and your faith in Me will overcome all difficulties.

195.

Lord Jesus—3/10/95

In the love of God you will find all you need. All your wants and all your desires are fulfilled in My love. So look to Me for everything and it is yours. Just trust, believe, and follow.

Vision—3/11/95—Vision at Mass of Host with red cross through it dripping blood.

Lord Jesus—3/11/95

Blood of Bloods,
Bread of Breads,
Love of Loves.
The Eucharist.

Lord Jesus—3/11/95

Showered in Blood, the Blood of your Savior.
Showered in Love, the Blood of your Savior.
Showered in Grace, the Blood of your Savior.
Immersed in Blood, the Blood of your Savior.
Immersed in Forgiveness, the Blood of your Savior.
Immersed in Mercy, the Blood of your Savior.
Cleansed in Blood, the Blood of your Savior.
Cleansed in Redemption, the Blood of your Savior.
Cleansed in Salvation, the Blood of your Savior.

The Holy Spirit—3/11/95

The Hand of God is upon all, the Hand of God is within all, the Hand of God guides all. Take God's Hand and be welcomed in Heaven.

The Holy Spirit—3/11/95

A step closer to God is a step further away from evil, and a step closer to God is a step nearer to your true self.

Vision—3/11/95—Vision at Divine Mercy Center during Exposition of the Sacrament, of Jesus with Our Lady looking over His right shoulder.

God, The Father—3/12/95

In a time of confusion, Jesus makes all clear; in a time of concern, Jesus makes all secure; in a time of turmoil, Jesus makes all calm. Trust Jesus and all will be well; trust Jesus and you will have no worries; trust Jesus and you will have no doubts. Just trust Jesus and find My love waiting for you.

The Holy Spirit—3/12/95

Ascending the stairway to Heaven is a hard climb but when you reach the top you find it was well worth the struggle. You find, looking back, that each step was guided by God; even when you stumbled, God was there to show you the value of overcoming each hurdle. Each time you struggled to your feet to carry on the climb, it was Jesus taking your hand and helping you up. Remember this when times are difficult and also remember when times are good.

God, The Father—3/13/95

After a long time mankind has reached an era of almost complete acceptance of sin. There are those who see sin for what it is, but they are not many. Many people see nothing wrong with what happens morally, ethically, spiritually. Many people listen to clever arguments and say that it sounds reasonable so it must be all right. All these clever arguments

do, is mask the evil of sin; all these clever arguments
do, is confuse the truth; all these clever arguments
do, is deceive. Mankind is so simple, that he is easy
to deceive; mankind is so lost, he is easy to show
the wrong way; and mankind is so self-centered, he
is easy to flatter and increase in pride. After a long
time mankind has become a heavy burden on My
Heart, a burden that needs to be lifted. Jesus now
asks all to change, asks all to be what they were
created to be, asks all to become God's children
again. Listen to My Son and save yourselves the pain
that comes, and comes soon.

Lord Jesus—3/13/95

> Slumber of Peace,
> Slumber of Joy,
> Slumber of Love,
> When you sleep with Me.

God, The Father—3/15/95

Humbleness leads to God and God leads to
humbleness.

Love brings you to God and God brings you love.

Faith strengthens you in God and God
strengthens your faith.

God, The Father—3/15/95

Among those who do My work are those who
remain in the background, working quietly, do not
forget them, always praise them for they often receive
little recognition. Always lift them in your prayers to
Me and always thank them for doing My work.

God, The Father—3/17/95 (Feast of St. Patrick)

A Son of Mine celebrates today.
A Son of Mine is thanked today.
A Son of Mine is praised today.
What a special Son,
Who by His Sacrifice for Me,
Brought so many to Me.

God, The Father—3/17/95

Long ago, My Son Jesus came to the world. He came in love and He came to bring hope and forgiveness to all. No one who listened to His words truly understood what He said and what He brought for mankind. Today those who read His words often put their personal interpretations into His Word and then proclaim it as the Lord's word.

Often these interpretations are wrong, often they lead from God instead of to God, often they are filled with man's pride or man seeking power or glory, often they denounce what Jesus actually said. To understand Jesus' Word is not possible without the help of God's Holy Spirit. Those who are theologians need to pray for God's guidance, need to be humble, and need to be very careful that they do not give the wrong meanings to Jesus' Word.

Remember, if an interpretation goes against the Commandments, against love, against the Sacraments, against prayer, against the Mother of God, against the Saints, then it is wrong; even if it is a little wrong, it is still wrong and must be prayed over so that My Son's true meaning can be seen. Today many do not do this, today many accept little changes, little wrongs and then they accept evil.

God, The Father—3/17/95

A lost generation needs guidance, a lost generation needs help, a lost generation needs saving. Jesus brings all of these, Jesus will rescue mankind and Jesus will lead mankind to His Father in Heaven.

199.

Lord Jesus—3/18/95

Warmth of love, heart of joy, spirit of kindness; if you have these you have humility.

Giving of self, taking to others, bringing of hope; if you have these you have humility.

Emptying of needs, filling of heart, opening of self; if you have these you have humility.

Seek them, find them, and follow them to Me.

Our Lady—3/18/95

Children of the world are the treasure of the future. Children of the world are God's children. Children of the world are for all to love.

Children of mankind are children of God. Children of mankind are God's gifts. Children of mankind are God's love.

Children of the world are so precious. Children of the world are so pure. Children of the world are so in need of love.

God, The Father—3/19-95

A child born in Love is a precious being; a child born in God is a precious Gift and a child born in Mercy is a precious Savior. Jesus is that Child.

Vision—3/20/95—Vision after communion of a boat in stormy waters; Jesus was steering it and I was lying on the floor, frightened. Jesus said, "Trust in Me." Then a Host appeared high in the sky shining white and the waters were calmed. Jesus said, "Find peace and calm in Me."

God, The Father—3/20/95

If giving to your children brings you such pleasure and joy, imagine then how much the Father in Heaven wants to give you, for it brings Him great pleasure and joy as you are His child.

God, The Father—3/20/95

Pleasure of love, pleasure of fatherly care, pleasure of giving. This is the pleasure the Father gets when His children accept His gifts.

Pleasure of sharing, pleasure of hoping, pleasure of filling with Him; this is the pleasure the Father gets when you trust in Him.

Pleasure of pleasures, pleasure of returned love, pleasure of union in Jesus; this is the pleasure the Father gets when you believe in Him.

God, The Father—3/20/95

Lost along the way are many of mankind, lost along the way are many who cannot see this.

Lost along the way are those who deny God.

Lord Jesus—3/22/95

Words of love for all, gifts of love for all, Jesus for all.

Light of God for all, love of God for all, Jesus for all.

Heart of God for all, hope of God for all, Jesus for all.

Lord Jesus—3/23/95

Under strain, under stress, under difficulties, stand under My shadow and all will be well.

ttt

God, The Father—3/23/95

My dear little ones, My heart is open to you, My love awaits you and My Spirit longs to fill you. If you look within yourself you will find that your heart awaits Mine, your love opens you to My love and your spirit needs to be touched by My Spirit. If you look within the Eucharistic Host you will find all this there for you in My Son Jesus.

God, The Father—3/24/95

At one with Me, at one with My Son, at one with My Spirit can be achieved by receiving the Sacraments and by praying. Receive and pray often and become one in God's love.

God, The Father—3/24/95

Bowing down before your God in adoration and worship is the most important act of love that you can offer Me. When you do this you become Mine for Eternity.

God, The Father—3/24/95

The truth is sometimes forgotten; the truth, though, is still the truth. The way is sometimes not seen but it is still the way. The light is sometimes blocked but it is still the light.

God is God, Jesus is God, and the Spirit is God; if mankind does not believe, it does not change the facts; they still remain true. The Truth, the Light and the Way are Jesus whether or not mankind chooses to believe. Jesus is the only way to Heaven whether or not mankind agrees.

A Divine Mystery revealed to mankind, a Divine Light given to mankind, and a Divine Mercy shown to mankind. Accept the Truth for it is fact, accept the Way for it is the only way, and accept the Light for it is God's Light.

Vision—3/25/95—Just after receiving communion, Jesus came to me with a rose in His hands. He dropped the rose into my hands and as I closed them they were pierced, each with a thorn. I opened my hands and the rose fell onto my feet, piercing each of them with a thorn. My hands and feet then started to bleed.

Lord Jesus—3/25/95

    Rose of Love, Gift of Joy.
    Rose of Love, Gift of the Savior.
    Rose of Love, Gift of Forgiveness.
    Thorn of Redemption, saving Grace.
    Thorn of Redemption, saving Love.
    Thorn of Redemption, saving God.
    Flower of Mercy, Jesus Christ, Son of God.
    Flower of Mercy, Jesus Christ, Son of the Lord.
    Flower of Mercy, Jesus Christ, Son of Mary.

God, The Father—3/27/95

Along the path to Heaven you will find many joys and many loves. Along this path to Heaven you will find My Son Jesus guiding, helping, and filling you with My Spirit.

God, The Father—3/27/95

Mirrored in your soul is the light of Jesus which you should reflect into others.
Mirrored in your heart is the love of Jesus which you should give to others.
Mirrored in your spirit is the Spirit of Jesus which you should bring to others.

God, The Father—3/27/95

Roman emperors could not stop the love of Jesus spreading.

Communism cannot stop the love of Jesus spreading.

Nationalism cannot stop the love of Jesus spreading.

Nothing can stop the love of Jesus spreading, for it is in every man's heart and soul.

They only need to accept it.

God, The Father—3/28/95

Children are a gift, a gift to mankind.

Children are sweet and innocent until they are taught not to be.

Children are what all mankind should try to be, then mankind will become the gift of love it was meant to be.

Our Lady—3/28/95

A child was born in Bethlehem, a child of Love.

A child was born in Bethlehem, a child who is Love.

A child was born in Bethlehem, a child who is God.

Our Lady—3/28/95

Jesus, so sweet is my Son,
Jesus, so sweet is my Lord,
Jesus, so sweet is God.

Our Lady—3/28/95

As I sat at the table with my son Jesus at the wedding feast in Cana, I knew this would be a special moment in my son's life on earth. When the water was changed to wine my son showed the world who He truly was. My son Jesus showed that God was waiting to help man in his time of need. Jesus showed that God could supply all that man needed; Jesus showed that God only wanted to help mankind.

What Jesus did on that day was to show that the water and the wine were a symbol of the water and wine of love that were to flow from His side on the Cross. That, just as He changed the water into wine, He could change man's hearts from sin to love by washing their spirits clean in His everlasting mercy flowing from His side. Jesus' first public miracle was to change water into wine, Jesus' everlasting miracle is to change mankind from evil to good.

Our Lady—3/28/95

Love is as real as you are.
Love is as sound as you are.
Love is as special as you are.
For you and all mankind are made from love to be love.

Our Lady—3/29/95

A flower grows in sunlight and so it is with you, you grow in My Son's light.

A flower blooms in spring and so it is with you, you bloom in the spring of love that flows from My Son's Heart.

A flower reaches its full potential before it returns to where it came from, so it is with you, you will reach your full potential before you return home to Heaven.

The Holy Spirit—3/28/95—(smell of roses)

Rose of love, Heart of Jesus.
Bud of beauty, Heart of Jesus.
Flower of glory, Heart of Jesus.
Fragrance of joy, Heart of God.
Perfume of happiness, Heart of God.
Aroma of love, Heart of God.
Scent of love, Heart of the Spirit.
Petal of fire, Heart of the Spirit.
Arrangement of gifts, Heart of the Spirit.

Vision—3/29/95—Seven candles in a holder with Jesus standing behind it. The words, "The Light of God" were said by Jesus.

The Holy Spirit—3/30/95

Following truth, love, and joy means following Jesus.
Following lies, hate, and anger means following evil.
The difference is so clear, why doesn't mankind recognize it?
The difference is so great, why doesn't man see it and the difference is so wide apart, how does man confuse it?

God, The Father—3/30/95

Father of man, Father of the universe, Father of creation.
Father of truth, Father of hope, Father of love.
Father of God, Father of the Spirit, Father of Jesus.
Father who is God.

God, The Father—3/30/95

Father, one with the Son, one with the Spirit.
One God, one love, one truth.
Three reflections of God, Three individuals yet three who are one, one God who loves all.

The Holy Spirit—3/30/95

Formed in love, formed to be love, formed for love, mankind.
Made in Heaven, made in love, made in hope, mankind.
Created by Truth, created by Love, created by God, mankind.

God, The Father—3/31/95

A Child of Love was born almost 2000 years ago,
A Child of Hope came to mankind,
A Child of Truth brought Himself to save.
This Child was Jesus, this Child is God, and this Child is Love.

God, The Father—3/31/95

God created man and then from man God came forth to save. What a mystery, what a divine revelation, what a gift to mankind.

God, The Father—3/31/95

When the world will look to the truth and accept it instead of accepting lies, then peace will come to earth. Mankind seems so willing to accept and welcome lies and deceit into its life, even when lies are so obvious that all can see they are wrong. Look at the times mankind accepts murder as being acceptable, be it in retribution, in war, in love of your country. Murder is never acceptable, but many, oh so many, see it as so.

How many people look upon those in other countries being tortured or maimed and say they are inferior anyway, so it doesn't really matter? The truth is, all are equal and it does matter, but this truth is often ignored. How many times do people accept others starving and say it is their own fault and do nothing to help? These same people exploit the starving by taking their resources, their wealth, their inheritance and using them as if they belong only to the wealthy nations.

The truth is, the resources in the world are for all equally and should be shared among the family of mankind. How many more examples there are of denying the truth, it is endless the way mankind covers and hides the truth. The truth is God and to deny the truth in any form is to deny God, and to deny God is to accept the evil one. Open your eyes now and live to the truth, live to love and live with God.

Lord Jesus—4/1/95

Blood of bloods, shed on the Cross.
Love of loves, given on the Cross.
Heart of hearts, opened on the Cross.
Peace of peace, found in the Cross.
Truth of truths, shown in the Cross.
Mercy of mercies, placed in the Cross.
Way of ways, given through the Cross.
Path of paths, shown through the Cross.
Heaven of heavens, opened through the Cross.

Lord Jesus—4/1/95

A crown was placed on My head in mockery but this crown was greater than all the kingdoms on earth for the crown was the crown of Love. A cross was placed on My back and this cross was meant to be a cross of shame, it became the cross of Glory, for this cross showed how great was God's love for mankind.

Nails were placed through My hands and feet; these nails were there to increase My suffering; these nails became a sign of My everlasting love for mankind by opening My body and bringing forth My Blood of Forgiveness. A spear pierced My side to ensure My death; this spear became the instrument that opened My Sacred Heart to shower mankind in God's mercy.

†††

Lord Jesus—4/2/95

Overflowing with My love is the Eucharist.
Overflowing with My healing gift is the Eucharist.
Overflowing with Myself is the Eucharist.

Lord Jesus—4/2/95

Promises today seem to mean little,
Vows today seem to mean little, and
Oaths before God seem to mean little.
Promises should only be given if they are to be kept.
Vows today should only be made if they are to be held true.
Oaths before God should only be said if they are to be lived by.

God, The Father—4/3/95

Changing from weak to strong means giving yourself completely to Jesus.
Changing from strong to weak means giving yourself completely to Jesus.
Changing from yourself first to others first means giving yourself completely to Jesus, and
Changing from sin to good means giving yourself completely to Jesus.
Give yourself in weakness to find the strength in Jesus to overcome sin.

God, The Father—4/3/95

Standing by the side of Jesus is His most loving Mother.
Holding the hand of Jesus is His most precious Mother.
Sharing the love of Jesus is His most giving Mother.
The precious love that Mary gives is the love of Jesus.

Vision—4/3/95—At Mass, Our Lady came to me with the Baby Jesus in her arms and the words "Queen of Mothers" appeared.

Lord Jesus—4/4/95

Search for your true self when you pray.
Look for your true feelings when you pray, and find God when you pray.

God, The Father—4/5/95

Taken within, the Host becomes the Lord Jesus' healing power.
Taken within, the Host becomes Jesus' healing love.
Taken within, the Host becomes one with you and you become one with Jesus.

God, The Father—4/5/95

Taken in trust, taken in faith, taken in truth, The Word of God.
Taken with hope, taken with belief, taken with humility, The Word of God.
Taken to be true, taken to be love, taken to be healing, The Word of God.

God, The Father—4/6/95

Merciful Heart of Jesus, Loving Heart of Jesus, Precious Heart of Jesus.
In His mercy, Jesus loves everyone and holds all precious.
Mercy is in the center of Jesus' Heart, Mercy is in the center of Jesus' Soul, Mercy is in the center of Jesus' Divinity, Jesus is Mercy.
Divine Heart, Divine Soul, Divine Spirit, Jesus.

God, The Father—4/7/95

The Soul of the Savior is the Savior of souls.
The Heart of the Redeemer is the Redeemer of hearts.
The Spirit of the Rescuer is the Rescuer of spirits.

God, The Father—4/7/95

Father of Forgiveness, Bringer of peace, God.
Son of salvation, Savior of man, God.
Spirit of freedom, Fire of heaven, God.

Lord Jesus—4/8/95

Under a bush I sat with My disciples discussing
the truth of God. As John leaned on My shoulder
and fell asleep, the love of My Father filled him and
kept him childlike. As I looked into his face I saw
the innocence, the faith and the love that all mankind
should have. John had these with him throughout his
life as a gift from God to lead others home. John,
in his youth, angelic, and in his life a saint.

Lord Jesus—4/8/95

Truth is a powerful weapon,
Faith is the ammunition, and
Hope is the aim.
Fire, the truth with faith and hope.

Lord Jesus—4/10/95

With the Arm of God around your shoulder to show
you the way, how can you be afraid?
With the Heart of God open wide for you, how can
you fear? With the Hand of God upon your soul, how
can you not succeed?

Lord Jesus—4/10/95

Living by the Bread of Life, is the true way to live.

Living by the Wine of Forgiveness, is the best way to live.

Living by the Fountain of Love, is the right way to live.

I am the Bread of Life, I am the Wine of Forgiveness, and

I am the Fountain of Love. I am Jesus.

God, The Father—4/10/95

A feast of love can be found in the Eucharist.

A feast of joy can be found in the Truth.

A feast of mercy can be found in Jesus' suffering.

The Eucharist is the truth of Jesus' merciful suffering.

God, The Father—4/12/95

My Son Jesus took all the pain and all the suffering of His passion so that My children could return home to Me.

My Son Jesus took all of mankind's sins and all of mankind's sorrow into His Heart so that evil could be defeated.

My Son Jesus took all mankind's needs and desires into His Soul so that they could be fulfilled by His Father.

Now Jesus opens his Heart and Soul to mankind again and once more shows how passionate is His love for My children.

Now Jesus suffers again to wash away mankind's sins and sorrow. Now my Son Jesus says to mankind, "I love you, now love Me."

God, The Father—4/13/95

Jesus suffered, Jesus died, Jesus rose again.
Jesus lived, Jesus died, Jesus lives again.
Jesus loved, Jesus died, Jesus lives eternally.
Jesus suffered for love, Jesus died in love,
Jesus lives eternally as Love.

God, The Father—4/13/95

Droplets of blood ran into My Son's eyes.
Tears of love ran down My Son's cheeks.
Rivers of mercy flowed through My Son's heart.
Streams of forgiveness flowed out of My Son's soul.
Oceans of saving grace gushed forth from My
Son's wounds.
Waves of God's Glory gushed outward from My
Son's sacrifice.

God, The Father—4/13/95

A yoke of sin hangs on the shoulders of mankind,
lift this yoke and replace it with the love of Jesus
which has no weight except the weight of joy.

God, The Father—4/14/95

Flowing in the breeze on Calvary that morning was
the Spirit of Forgiveness.
Floating through the air on Calvary that day was
the Mercy of God.
Filling the atmosphere on Calvary that moment was
the Glory of God.

213.

Lord Jesus—4/14/95

As I walked along the path of Calvary, I looked into the faces of those around Me. I saw those who hated Me, I saw those who mocked Me, I saw those who beat Me, and I saw those who loved Me. Today I look and I see the same. Those who hate Me, denounce Me. Those who mock Me, jest over Me. Those who beat Me, abuse My servants. Those who love Me, still love Me through all this. Those who love Me still mourn for those who do not understand, and those who love Me are loved by Me.

God, The Father—4/14/95

My Son died for mankind,
My Son lived for mankind, and
My Son lives forever offering mankind His Love.

God, The Father—4/14/95

Cross of Love, Cross of Forgiveness, Cross of God.
Cross of Truth, Cross of Redemption, Cross of God.
Cross of Hope, Cross of the Savior, Cross of God.
The Love, the Truth, and the Hope that is found in the Redeeming Forgiveness of the Savior.

God, The Father—4/14/95

Hanging by the nails tearing His flesh, My son gave His all for mankind. The pain that racked His body did not stop His love for mankind; it magnified it.

The abuse showered upon My Son did not stop His forgiveness flowing from His soul; it deepened it.

The humiliation hurled at My Son did not stop His redeeming sacrifice; it glorified it.

The final breath My Son took did not end His suffering; it endures as long as mankind sins.

✝✝✝

Our Lady—4/15/95

Trust in the Lord for He trusts in you. Accept your faults and weaknesses as the Lord accepts them, and together with Jesus overcome them.

Lord Jesus—4/16/95

A long time ago the world was shown how much God loves mankind.
A long time ago the world was shown how much God would give for mankind.
A long time ago the world was shown how much God asked from mankind.
God gives all and asks for little in return.
Mankind takes all and gives little in return.
Mankind needs to give a little more to receive completeness in God.

Lord Jesus—4/16/95

By the lake as the water lapped upon the sand, I sat and watched My disciples in their boat. They had caught nothing and were wondering if they would. Then they saw their Lord by the fire on the shore and they did not know Me. I directed them to cast their nets out again and when the nets were pulled in, they were filled with fish. Peter then knew Me and in his joy, jumped into the water to come to Me. He completely abandoned all else to come to his Lord, whom he loved.

The lesson that day was to trust in Me, for without Me you cannot succeed. Follow My Word and your catch will be great, follow yourself and your catch will be empty. To do this you must abandon yourself joyfully in Me and be prepared to commit yourself fully to Me.

Lord Jesus—4/16/95

Flogged for man's failures, pierced for man's pride, and crucified for man's crimes. The failure to love God, the pride of putting man before God, and the crime of disobeying God.

Lord Jesus—4/16/95

The world is My love, the people are My children, and their spirits are My treasure.
I love My children and treasure their spirits in My Merciful Heart.

Lord Jesus—4/16/95

The world is My glory, My glory to give to the Father.
The world is My gift, My gift for the Father.
The world is My joy, My joy to offer to the Father.
My glorious gift of My children's love brings joy to the Father and My Father loves to return glorious joy to Our children.

God, The Father—4/18/95

A child of Heaven came to earth to declare the good news.
A child of Heaven came to earth to promise freedom from sins.
A child of Heaven came to earth to proclaim the Glory of God.
A child who is the Father's Son,
A child who is the Spirit's Son,
A child who is the Son of God.

Lord Jesus—4/18/95

Sunshine brightens the day.
Sonshine brightens the spirit.
Sunshine helps the plants grow.
Sonshine helps the soul grow.
Sunshine brings light into dark.
Sonshine brings fire into being.

Our Lady—4/19/95

Flights of Angels surround the Lord singing His praise and glory.
Flights of Angels encompass the Lord offering Him their love.
Flights of Angels together with the saints fall in adoration of the Lord.
The joy in Heaven of the Lord's saving grace given to mankind knows no end, for all in Heaven want mankind with them in God's love.

Vision—4/19/95—After Communion, vision of Jesus offering His left hand to me. As I took it I entered the wound in His hand. Inside the wound were Angels flying around and as I went deeper, Jesus appeared and said, "My wounds are the doorway to Heaven."

God, The Father—4/21/95

No circumstances justify denying the truth.
No circumstances justify altering the facts.
No circumstances justify sin.

Lord Jesus—4/21/95

Under My wing you will learn to fly.
Under My shadow you will learn to shine.
Under My cross you will learn to give.

†††

Lord Jesus—4/21/95

The cross showered all with My love.
The cross showered all with My gifts.
The cross showered all with My spirit.
Mankind only needs to stand by Me and all this is his.
The spear pierced My heart bringing forth a river of mercy.
The spear pierced My being bringing forth a river of hope.
The spear pierced My dead body bringing forth a river of truth.
Mankind only needs to accept this and all is his.
The grave held My body for only a moment.
The grave held My soul only at rest.
The grave held My spirit only at peace.
Mankind only needs to acknowledge this and eternity is his.

Lord Jesus—4/22/95

The cross, the spear, and the grave are signs that in God's love all can be overcome and that all is there, if only mankind would love God.

Lord Jesus—4/22/95

Roaming the world looking for love is the Heart of the Savior.
Walking next to all mankind is the Spirit of the Lord.
Reaching out to each person is the Love of God.
Take the hand that is offered,
Take the love that is there, and
Take a step to eternal joy.

Lord Jesus—4/22/95

Drops of eternal joy are placed into mankind's soul.
Veils of sorrow are placed over them.
Gifts of eternal love are placed into mankind's spirit,
Veils of hate and anger are covering them.
Truths of God are placed in mankind's heart,
Veils of sin are hiding them.
Lift the veils and be free in God's love, joy, and truth.

Lord Jesus—4/25/95

The blood that dripped from My wounds with every heart beat was the grace I gave mankind, the grace of My love.
The life that ebbed away with every heart beat was the grace I gave mankind, the grace of showing that this life is secondary to eternal life.
The cry that came from My mouth as I hung there dying was a grace for mankind, a grace for the Father's forgiveness.

God, The Father—4/26/95

Women of God are oh, so special, Women of God are oh, so loving, Women of God are so dear to Me.
When Jesus walked this earth, He walked it because a woman loved God completely.
When Jesus carried the cross, His face was cleansed with the love of a woman for her God.
When Jesus hung on the cross, the women who loved God remained with Him. Arising from death, the Lord Jesus first showed a woman His glory.
After ascending to Heaven, the Lord Jesus assumed a woman into Heaven, a woman who was to become Queen of Heaven.
On the final day the Lord Jesus will have a woman at His side to defeat evil.
Throughout time, God loves women with the deepest of loves, and throughout spiritual life, God sees women as He sees men.

Woman and man the same but different, what a divine mystery. Woman and man both created to love God and each other.

Woman and man both here to do God's work but in different ways, both ways very special to God.

God, The Father—4/26/95

Waking in the arms of Jesus,
Opening your eyes to the love of Jesus,
Walking in the light of Jesus.
Every moment should be like this,
Every moment, a moment for Jesus.

Lord Jesus—4/26/95

Love becomes complete in God,
Love becomes complete when you see what it truly is.
Love is everything and everything comes from love.
Love created all, so all must be love.
God created, so God is Love.
God made man to be love and to love.
Love denied is God denied and God denied is evil accepted, even when it does not seem so.
Love denied is a denial of eternal life and love denied is an invitation to hate, greed, anger, pain, suffering, and sin.
Love denied is a sin for it is a denial of God who is Love.

Lord Jesus—4/26/95

Love waits, love is patient, love trusts.
Love Me by waiting patiently and trusting in Me, your Lord God, Jesus Christ.

God, The Father—4/26/95

Love of mankind, is what you must show all mankind.
Love of the Church, is what you must show all the Church.
Love of Jesus, is what you must show always.

God, The Father—4/26/95

Playing to win is not playing.
Playing for enjoyment is playing.
For playing must be fun or it is not playing.

God, The Father—4/26/95

A fruit should be tasted and enjoyed.
A fruit should be picked when it is ripe.
A fruit should be placed on show so that the goodness of its tree is seen.

Lord Jesus—4/26/95

Opening others to My Word is not easy.
Opening others to My Love is difficult.
Opening others to My Mercy is a struggle. It can be no other way, for My work is always hard.

Lord Jesus—4/27/95

Trusting, believing, and following, is the way of My friends.
Trusting I am there to answer your prayers, believing I am by your side at all times, and following My Light as it brings you to those in need.

Lord Jesus—4/27/95

Thorns, nails, and a spear could not stop My Mercy; they magnified it.

Pain, suffering, and humiliation cannot stop your work, they can only glorify it.

Love, faith, and hope can strengthen your shoulders for the cross you have to carry.

Lord Jesus—4/27/95

Truth will always win, so always be truthful. It is understandable to make mistakes for this is your humanity; those who cannot accept this, close their eyes and their hearts to the truth.

Lord Jesus—4/27/95

True hearts belong to Jesus,
True spirits belong to God,
True souls belong to Heaven.

Lord Jesus—4/27/95

Breath of Truth, Breath of Forgiveness,
Breath of Mercy, Breath of Love.
This is the last Breath I took on the Cross.

Sigh of Sorrow, Sigh of Tenderness,
Sigh of Affection, Sigh of Love.
This is the last Sigh I gave on the Cross.

Whisper of Grace, Whisper of Majesty,
Whisper of Eternity, Whisper of Love.
This is the last Whisper I spoke on the Cross.

I breathed a sigh that whispered God's love to the world.

I sighed a breath that whispered God's forgiveness to the world, and I whispered a sigh that breathed new life into mankind.

Lord Jesus—4/27/95

The Mother of Jesus is such a special mother. Sweet Mother, who devoted all her life to God, sweet Mother who gave all to God. My Mother, by giving birth to the Son of God placed herself above all others. When God chose Mary, He chose her before she was born, He chose her to be immaculate. He chose her to be the new Eve, He chose her because she was pure.

Mary who was free from sin unlike any of mankind before her and unlike any of mankind since. Mary, My mother, so innocent, so pure, so free from sin.

The act of giving birth to the Son of God lifts My mother above all others. The act of nurturing, caring for, and giving herself completely to Me as I grew, lifts Mary, My mother, above all others. The act of walking the way of the cross with Me without begging for My freedom, without complaining, and without blaming God for My suffering, lifts My mother above all others.

The act of laying My Body in the tomb and trusting in God that I would return lifts My mother above all others. The act of comforting and strengthening My disciples as they waited uncertain of their future after I ascended to Heaven lifted My mother above all others.

When I assumed My mother into Heaven, this lifted My mother above all others. When My mother is ignored it hurts Me, as it would hurt man if his mother was ignored.

Imagine a friend was visiting, and your mother welcomed him into your house but he totally ignored her and came straight to you, wouldn't you be offended? Imagine if your mother offered your friends gifts but they turned their backs on her, wouldn't you be offended? Imagine if your friends came to your house injured and your mother offered them care and comfort but they ignored her and only asked for your help, wouldn't you be offended?

It is the same with My mother; when she is ignored I am offended. When she is turned away, I am offended. When she is spurned, I am offended. My mother was chosen by God and My mother is

223.

favored by God, so show her the respect she deserves;
the respect the Mother of God deserves. When you
pray through My mother you pray to ask for her help,
her intercession, her asking God to help you. God,
who asked so much from Mary longs to give so
much through her. Mary, a favored human, not God,
but oh so special!

God, The Father—4/27/95

Eating of My Son's Body is the true food of life.
Drinking of My Son's Blood is the sweetest drink
of Life.
Filling yourself with My Son's Body and Blood brings
you true Life.

Lord Jesus—4/28/95

Friendship means Love, friendship means Trust, and
friendship means Hope. Your hopes are fulfilled when
you trust in My Love.

Lord Jesus—4/29/95

Love of others is a gift, love of self is a sin.
Love of others is a grace, love of self is a barrier.
Love of others is a joy, love of self is pride.
Love others and find the joy that gracefully
becomes a gift that brings you to God.

The Holy Spirit—4/29/95

Flower of Heaven, Fruit of Love.
Rose of God, Fragrance of Love.
Bouquet of Grace, Gift of Love.
Jesus, the rose whose bouquet brings souls into
flower.

God, The Father—4/29/95

The blood drips down My Son's face to form a mask of love. The blood runs down My Son's arms to form an embrace of love. The blood flows from My Son's side to form a river of love. Run to the river and let the love flow into your soul. Run to the river and let the love fill your spirit so that you become the face of Jesus' love. Run to the river and let the love wash your hands clean to become the embrace of Jesus' love.

God, The Father—4/29/95

As I watched My Son, sweet Jesus, live His life on Earth I was filled with happiness. As I watched Him bring God's Love, God's Word, and God's forgiveness to My children, I was filled with joy. As I watched Him show mankind the way home to Heaven, I was filled with mercy. Jesus gave to Me what was Mine and I returned to Him what was His. Jesus gave to Me Himself and I gave Him My love.

Lord Jesus—4/29/95

A child remains inside a man throughout his life and a man needs to be inside the child. To be a child is to be loved, so always be childlike.

Our Lady—4/29/95

Lost children become confused, lost children are easily led, lost children need understanding and compassion. Lost children seek the truth, lost children are easily deceived, lost children take any hand. Lost children are not to blame, lost children follow in hope, lost children need to be found.

Our Lady—4/29/95

How easy it is for the evil one to take My children away with half truths, half reasons. The ridiculous can be made to look the truth. Mankind's souls are from God's love and are created to return to God in Heaven. The souls of mankind are not created to be animals or created to live over and over as humans. Each soul, each spirit is unique and when it is given its human body this body is unique to this soul.

There are only two choices, the choice of Heaven or Hell, any other choice is only the choice that leads to Hell, any other choice is a deception from the evil one. Any other choice is a lie. Has anyone except the Lord Jesus come back to life and shown what follows death? Has anyone other than the Lord Jesus foretold His death and Resurrection? Has anyone except the Lord Jesus defeated death?

This is the proof that the Lord Jesus is the true Son of God and is the true way to Heaven. Has any other sent the Holy Spirit to fill His children with the gifts and graces of God? Has anyone but the Lord Jesus said you will heal and raise the dead in His name and fulfilled His promise? Has anyone else except the Lord Jesus said demons will flee from His name, and fulfilled this promise?

Has anyone else made so many saints that showed His love? Has anyone else appeared over and over for nearly two thousand years to proclaim God's love? Has anyone else performed so many miracles? Has anyone else lived eternally? And has anyone else loved man so that He gave His life for the forgiveness of their sins? Who else has done these things? Who else has proclaimed the greatness of God with His every breath? Who else?

God, The Father—5/1/95

Finding peace within, is as easy as finding Jesus. Finding love within, is as pleasant as finding Jesus. Finding truth within, is as clear as finding Jesus. Jesus is peace, love, and truth. So, when you find My Son, Jesus, you find these.

Lord Jesus—5/1/95—(after crying in Confession)

Tears of love are released in the Sacraments, tears of sorrow are shed in Confession, and tears of joy are wept in the understanding of your weakness.

Lord Jesus—5/1/95

Your heart opens to expose its true self, your heart opens to show your true love, and your heart opens to bring its flower into bloom.

God, The Father—5/2/95

A man's heart can be like stone or a man's heart can be like flowers, one dead and unfeeling, the other alive and fragrant. Turn the stones into flowers with the touch of Jesus, and turn the flowers into bouquets with the love of Jesus.

God, The Father—5/2/95

The way to understand how life should be, is to understand what My Son Jesus said. My Son only ever spoke of love, love of God, love of fellow man, and love of yourself. To live by love means your whole life will be free of sin, for if you love, then you will never offend or hurt your God or your fellow man.

To live in love means that you treasure the love you receive from your God and your fellow man. To live by love means you accept all difficulties, all abuse, all rejection, and all adversities, and respond only by loving and loving more. To live with love means you live your life with Jesus, for He is love, My love.

227.

God, The Father—5/2/95

Love is My Son and My Son is Love.
Love is My Truth and My Truth is My Son.
Love is My Peace and My Peace is My Son.

God, The Father—5/2/95

Watching His Disciples praying, My Son longed to
show them what their prayers really were. The ones
who followed Jesus did not truly know what joy their
prayers brought to God. They did not know that I
listened on every word they spoke, every thought they
had, and every emotion they felt. They did not know
that every moment of their lives was a prayer that
Jesus offered to Me.

Jesus, from the time He chose His Apostles, offered
them as a gift to Me, His Father, a gift of love. Each
action they did was to glorify My Son and through
Jesus, glorify Me. It is only when you look back that
you see what they did with each action, each word.
It is only when you understand by the Spirit you see
the true meaning of their lives. Their lives guided by
Jesus so that throughout time mankind could see
God's will and God's message, and they are:

Love your God, love your fellow man and live a
life of love regardless of what others do to you. This
is a message of the Apostles, the message I sent
through My Son Jesus to show the way home to your
God in Heaven. The message that all should live by.
The message that is so clear, so obvious, and so true
that none should misunderstand it.

Lord Jesus—5/4/95

The strength you seek, you will find in the Eucharist,
the love you need, you will find in the Eucharist, and
the joy you desire, you will find in the Eucharist,
for I am the Eucharist.

Lord Jesus—5/4/95

The time of love is near, the time of love's joy comes, the time of love's fullness is in sight. The way will become clear, the way will become obvious, the way will become a vision of beauty. Take My strength and in time find the way; take time to seek My strength and find the way.

The Holy Spirit—5/5/95

The Hand of God brings peace to all,
The Hand of God brings love to all,
The Hand of God brings Jesus to all,
The Hand of God brings the peace and love that is Jesus.

Lord Jesus—5/6/95

Speaking of love means speaking of Jesus.
Speaking of life means speaking of Jesus.
Speaking of truth means speaking of Jesus.
Jesus is the truth that brings love to life, Jesus is the life that makes love true, and Jesus is the love that leads to true life.

Lord Jesus—5/6/95

Father of all nations, Father of all creation, Father of all mankind. The Father in Heaven created all nations to be one as the family of mankind. The Father in Heaven created all mankind to be one nation, the nation of God. The Father in Heaven created all for mankind so they could be a united nation of God's love.

God, The Father—5/7/95

When My Son Jesus returned to show mankind that life after death does exist, He also showed mankind so much more. When He spoke to the two Disciples on the road, He explained the Holy Scripture and by doing so said to mankind; "This is the Word of God, you should read it and understand it by the Grace of the Holy Spirit."

When Jesus explained it to these two they came to understand what the Holy Scripture really said, but it took God's helping hand for them to understand. It is the same for all mankind; they need the help of God truly to understand what Scripture says. It is the Holy Spirit that waits to help mankind see the truth in the Word.

When the Lord Jesus asked Thomas to put his hand into the Holy Wounds, what My Son was offering mankind was the Saving Grace that came from His suffering. Jesus was saying to all mankind, "Place yourself into My Wounds and be filled with My love and protection." What the Lord Jesus showed mankind was that His Wounds are there as a sign of love, a shelter of forgiveness, and a haven of peace for those who are prepared to reach out to touch His Wounds. What the Lord Jesus also did, with this act of Mercy, was to say it is all right to doubt for this is human, but once you are touched by Jesus' Wounds of Love, He will take your doubts away.

When the Lord Jesus came and ate with His friends, the Lord was saying, "I long to share My table with all My friends. I have a place for all My children where they can sit with Me and enjoy a feast of Love." What the Lord Jesus said when He prepared the fish on the shore, is that He prepares a food for all. A food that is His gift to His followers, a food that comes from His humility, a food that is an eternal feast that brings never-ending life.

What the Lord Jesus did when He offered the fish, was to offer Himself as food from the eternal sea of life in Heaven. What the Lord Jesus did when He walked with Peter alone, was to say to mankind, "I anoint this man to lead My children to My table in Heaven where with the Holy Spirit and the Father,

We will treasure them forever." What the Lord Jesus did when He asked John to wait behind, was to say: "Peter is the first and you are to follow and obey for he is My anointed."

What the Lord Jesus did, was to show that all those who followed in Peter's footsteps were His anointed and that no matter how close to God you were, He wanted you to follow and obey the Word of God's anointed vessel. What Jesus did on this day, was to confirm to all who would listen, to all who would see that He chooses His shepherd, not mankind. What Jesus showed through John, was that to love God meant to be humble and to follow God's wishes. What Jesus did on that day, was to set in stone, the stone that was Peter, His desire that all mankind follow in humility, His chosen one who was anointed to lead, lead in humility and love.

Today mankind needs to look and see if he is following this clear direction from Jesus, or if his pride keeps him from accepting God's anointed, God's chosen, God's shepherd who holds the keys that Peter passed on, and who is Jesus' chosen one.

God, The Father—5/8/95

A flower opens to show its Creator's glory; become that flower.

A flower gives its perfume to the world to show its Creator's love; become that flower.

A flower reaches for the sun and lives a life of beauty to show its Creator's joy; become that flower.

As you open your heart to Jesus, He gives you all you need to reach the hearts of others and open them to the Son.

Vision—5/8/95—Jesus came to me during Mass. Before communion, Jesus offered His Hands to me to show me His Wounds saying, "Look deep within My Wounds." As I did I could see many of the sins committed by man, e.g., the Jews in the gas chambers, people hacked to death, people fighting wars, committing murder, rape, homosexual acts, torture, abortions. Jesus said, "I carry the pain of this in My Wounds, look deeper." I saw Our Lady crying, looking down on the abortions saying, "My babies," with her hands open wide.

The Holy Spirit—5/8/95—(about Charismatics, Pentecostals, etc.)

Among those I have filled, are many who still deny My full truth. This does not stop Me filling them, it only stops them allowing My full love to flow through them. Think of your children when you give them gifts, and some of the gifts they do not like or want. They turn their backs on these gifts and it hurts you, but you do not stop offering them gifts, and you are happy when they accept them.

This is how it is with many; I offer them much but they only accept what they want, what suits their needs or their understanding. I offer them everything, but if they refuse some, I will not deny them what they accept. Quite the opposite is true. Often I fill them so full of what they accept, in the hope they will open themselves completely to My gifts.

Often these children, like all children, believe they have the answers to all and will not listen when their God wants to show them the truth. Are not most children like this? They often think they know better than their parents, only to find in hindsight how wrong they were. Open yourself completely; do not put any barrier between God and you; allow God's gifts to flow freely through you and see what wonders will happen.

Our Lady—5/9/95

Reaching out for love, reaching out for help and reaching out for understanding.

Most of my children need help to understand what love truly is. Most of my children need love to help them understand, and most of my children need to understand that love helps all. Most of my children need to understand that Jesus is love, and Jesus loves to help all.

Lord Jesus—5/10/95

Forgiveness not hate, love not loathing, true friendship not animosity, are My ways and they must become your ways.
To do My work you must imitate Me,
To do My work you must follow Me,
To do My work you must love as Me.

Lord Jesus—5/11/95

Feeding your soul with love is the only way to grow into the true self you were meant to be. The food for your soul is only found in the Eucharist for I am that food and I am the Bread of Life.

Lord Jesus—5/11/95

Sharing My warmth means giving yourself.
Sharing My love means giving yourself.
Sharing My truth means giving yourself.
Give My love warmly and always truthfully.

Lord Jesus—5/11/95

Freedom was given to mankind when I gave My life on the Cross.
The freedom I gave only needs to be accepted to be.
The freedom I gave is there for all to be redeemed.
The freedom I gave is an eternal gift that awaits all who accept it in love. The freedom I gave is the freedom of love.

Lord Jesus—5/12/95

Fruit of God is the fruit of love,
Fruit of love is Jesus.
Flower of God is the flower of mercy,
Flower of love is Jesus.
Gift of God is the gift of forgiveness,
Gift of God is Jesus.
Be fruitful and flower in the gifts that Jesus gives you through His Holy Spirit.

Lord Jesus—5/13/95

True friendship lasts, true friendship is forever, true friendship is found in Me.
True love lasts forever, true love never dies, true love is found in Me.
True hope lasts eternally, true hope is everlasting, true hope is found in Me.
I am a true friend who loves you eternally.
I am a true friend in whom you can place all your hopes and find eternal love, for
I am Jesus Christ your friend.
Trust Me, love Me, and find peace in Me.

Our Lady—5/13/95

As a mother, I look down upon my children with the love all mothers have for their families.
As a mother, I long to embrace my children and tell them that I love them.
As a mother, I long to spoil my children with little gifts of love.

As a mother, I long to show my children what is the safest and right path for them to walk.

As a mother, I look to the future for my children and hope that it will bring the best for them.

As a mother, I let my children walk their own way, but I give my gentle loving advice to guide them.

As a mother, I am hurt when my children are hurt, I am sad when my children are sad, and I am sorry when my children do wrong.

As a mother, I always forgive them, and as a mother, I always seek forgiveness for them.

As a mother, I always look to bringing my children home to their father, and as a mother, I always wait for my children to come to me.

As a mother, I always wonder when the next visit will be, and as a mother, I long for my children's love.

As a mother, I wait patiently for the day my children overcome their selfishness and become the true persons I know them to be.

As a mother, I long for the day when all my children come home safely, and together with the Father we can celebrate the family reunion.

Our Lady—5/13/95

Mankind, the family of God.
God, the Father of all.
Mankind, the family of Jesus.
Jesus, the Savior of all.
Mankind, the family of the Spirit.
The Holy Spirit, the giver of all.

Our Lady—5/13/95

Freedom in God in the only true freedom.
Freedom in God is the only true love.
Freedom in God is the only true choice.
Choose love freely and receive love freely.

††

(Conversation of 1/28/97—Editor and Ames)

Editor: Alan, we have three empty pages at the back of the book. Before we go to press, pray and see what God wants us to put there.

Alan: It has come to me that we should tell about Heaven. I will fax you something.

Editor: Alan, it looks good, but I think we should have an introduction.

Alan: This morning (1/29/97) Mother said the following:

Heaven, full of love.
Hell, full of hate.
Choose wisely.

Reference Our Lady gave for the message: *(Prov. 19:16— He who keeps the commandment is keeper of himself, but he who despises the word shall die.)*

Imagine Heaven

Lord Jesus—8/7/94

I will now tell you of Heaven. Imagine a place of warmth and light, full of laughter and happiness. Every moment is a moment of ecstasy. Every moment a moment of joy. Your every desire fulfilled, your every request completed. Your every thought happens. All around you are spirits of joy and happiness, who together with you, love, love, love.

All around are those you have loved and those who have loved you. All around is happiness and joy. A moment is a lifetime, so each lifetime is full of love. You feel so happy, all you can do is smile. You feel so happy, all you can do is laugh. You feel so happy, all you can do is love. The Lord is all around you filling your very being with Him...all glory and honor is God's, all praise is the Lord's. You know you will spend forever in happiness, forever in joy, forever in God.

How can I compare it to you? It is so glorious nothing compares.

Imagine you won all the riches in the world and every man, woman, child, and animal loved you dearly. Imagine the world turned at your command. Imagine the sea opened up for you to show you all its wonders. Imagine every living thing bowed down before you. Imagine you lived happy and healthy for a million years. Imagine everything you tasted, tasted wonderful. Imagine everything you touched felt wonderful. Imagine everything you saw was beautiful. Imagine you knew everything. Imagine you knew nothing but love. Imagine you knew nothing but feeling good.

Imagine life like that, then imagine a million times that...and you still cannot imagine Heaven. Imagine a never ending multiplication of that...and you still cannot see Heaven. Imagine that.

You Feel What You Never Thought Possible

Lord Jesus—10/22/95

What a glorious place full of love, full of peace, full of enjoyment. Think of the happiest moment in your life, and then magnify that a billion times, and it does not compare to the smallest of touches of Heaven. When you are in Heaven, you are so full of God's love you know nothing else except complete ecstasy...an ecstasy which increases and increases.

Each soul in heaven is a mirror of God's love, and so when you see each other you see God's love, and are lifted in ecstasy even more. Just when you think you have all the joy you could ever desire, the Father fills you with more and more. You become a light burning brighter and brighter in God's love. You come to understand this will never end, it will only increase as the Father has an unlimited supply of love to share. As you enter each doorway in Heaven, you find wonders and joys you could never have imagined. You find everyone in love with you, and you in love with them. You soar in unison with them in singing the praises of God, and as you do, you are filled with even more love from the Father.

All the saints you have heard of are there and you see the angels and archangels, and together you fly throughout eternity looking upon all the wonders God has made. You come to understand the joy of God in everything He has created. You see beautiful valleys filled with the most fragrant flowers. You see spirits of love waiting to play with you, waiting to share their love with you. You see mountains of golden light exploding into a cascade of light that touches you and fills you with joy.

You see rivers of so many beautiful colors, all flowing to join as a sea of wonderful fountains that, when you bathe in them, your whole being resounds with happiness. You see all around you lovely delicacies that, when you taste them, you are engulfed in the warmth of love.

As you take the hands of your companion saints in Heaven and look to the Father, your spirit explodes like a firework in joyful love. As the light from your spirit is touched by those around you, every spirit unites to become one with God, and then you feel what you never thought possible.

You feel all the love in eternity entering into you. You feel and see all the good things that have happened. You become part of all these things. You become part of all the love that has been shared among mankind, among the angels, and among the saints. You become part of every moment of love that has ever happened...and then you understand what Heaven truly is.